Threshold Concepts in Women's and Gender Studies: Ways of Seeing, Thinking, and Knowing

Threshold Concepts in Women's and Gender Studies: Ways of Seeing, Thinking, and Knowing is a textbook designed primarily for introduction to Women's and Gender Studies courses with the intent of providing both a skills- and concept-based foundation in the field. The text is driven by a single key question: "What are the ways of thinking, seeing, and knowing that characterize women's and gender studies and are valued by its practitioners?" Rather than taking a topical approach, *Threshold Concepts in Women's and Gender Studies* develops the key concepts and ways of thinking that students need in order to develop a deep understanding and to approach material like feminist scholars do, across disciplines. This book illustrates four of the most critical concepts in Women's and Gender Studies—the social construction of gender, privilege and oppression, intersectionality, and feminist praxis—and grounds these concepts in multiple illustrations.

Christie Launius directs and teaches in the Women's and Gender Studies program at the University of Wisconsin, Oshkosh. She has taught the introductory course for almost 20 years at six different institutions. She is also active in the field of working class studies; she edits *Working Class Notes,* the newsletter of the Working Class Studies Association, and became president of the association in 2014.

Holly Hassel has taught women's studies and English at the University of Wisconsin, Marathon County, one of the two-year campuses of the University of Wisconsin Colleges, for over a decade. Her work on teaching and learning in women's studies has been published in multiple books and journals. She is associate editor of the journal *Teaching English in the Two-Year College.*

Titles of Related Interest

Feminist Theory Reader: Local and Global Perspectives
Carole McCann and Seung-kyung Kim

Women Science, and Technology: A Reader in Feminist Science Studies,
Third Edition
Edited by Mary Wyer, Mary Barbercheck, Donna Cookmeyer,
Hatice Ozturk, and Marta Wayne

Transforming Scholarship: Why Women's and Gender Studies Students Are
Changing Themselves and the World, Second Edition
Michele Tracy Berger and Cheryl Radeloff

Reproduction and Society: Interdisciplinary Readings
Edited by Carole Joffe and Jennifer Reich

Gender Circuits: Bodies and Identities in a Technological Age,
Second Edition
Eve Shapiro

Pursuing Intersectionality, Unsettling Dominant Imaginaries
Vivian M. May

Threshold Concepts in Women's and Gender Studies

Ways of Seeing, Thinking, and Knowing

Christie Launius and Holly Hassel

Routledge
Taylor & Francis Group

NEW YORK AND LONDON

First published 2015
by Routledge
711 Third Avenue, New York, NY 10017

and by Routledge
2 Park Square, Milton Park, Abingdon, Oxon, OX14 4RN

Routledge is an imprint of the Taylor & Francis Group, an informa business

Library of Congress Cataloging-in-Publication Data
Threshold concepts in women's and gender studies : ways of seeing, thinking, and knowing / by Christie Launius and Holly Hassel.
    pages cm
 1. Women's studies. 2. Feminism. 3. Sex role. I. Hassel,
Holly. II. Title.
    HQ1180.L38 2015
    305.42—dc23
    2014030458

ISBN: 978-1-138-78879-4 (hbk)
ISBN: 978-1-138-78880-0 (pbk)
ISBN: 978-1-315-76515-0 (ebk)

Typeset in Adobe Caslon and Copperplate
by Apex Covantage, LLC

CONTENTS

This chapter focuses on distinctions between sex and gender, exploring how gender is socially constructed, and to what ends, as well as how social constructions of gender are shaped by issues of race, class, age, ability, and sexual identity.

Systems of privilege and oppression profoundly shape individual lives. This chapter explains how these systems play out via ideology and societal institutions, and are internalized by individuals.

Intersectionality is at the heart of feminist analysis. This chapter explores how different groups benefit from or are disadvantaged by institutional structures, as well as how overlapping categories of identity profoundly shape our experiences within institutions.

PREFACE

Threshold Concepts in Women's and Gender Studies: Ways of Seeing, Thinking, and Knowing is a textbook designed primarily for use in the introductory course in the field of Women's and Gender Studies (WGS) with the intent of providing both a skills- and concept-based foundation in the field. The text is driven by a single key question: "What are the ways of thinking, seeing, and knowing that characterize our field and are valued by its practitioners?" Through extensive review of the published literature, conversations with Women's and Gender Studies faculty across the University of Wisconsin System, and our own systematic research and assessment of student learning needs, we identified four of the most critical threshold concepts in Women's and Gender Studies:

- the social construction of gender
- privilege and oppression
- intersectionality
- feminist praxis

This textbook aims to introduce students to how these four concepts provide a feminist lens across the disciplines and outside the classroom. The term "threshold concept" is defined by Meyer and Land as a core disciplinary concept that is both troublesome and transformative. As they go on to explain, "A threshold concept can be considered as akin to a portal, opening up a new and previously inaccessible way of thinking about something. It represents a transformed way of understanding, or interpreting, or viewing something without which the learner cannot progress." A threshold concept is integrative, and when students cross the threshold and grasp a concept, "the hidden interrelatedness" of other concepts within that discipline becomes apparent (Cousin 4).

What Makes This Book Unique

The majority of WGS textbooks tend to be organized around the institutions that foster and reinforce gender hierarchies while also acknowledging the intersections of gender with race, class, and sexuality. Typical examples of these institutions include women and work, the family, media and culture, religion and spirituality, health and medicine, etc. Some focus exclusively on the U.S., while others integrate, to greater or lesser degrees, a global focus. Most also conclude with a chapter on activism. This approach privileges coverage of content over the disciplinary ways of knowing, seeing, and doing. These textbooks certainly introduce and employ these four threshold concepts, but often as a one-shot definition, with the assumption that students will come to understand the concepts' centrality through encountering them repeatedly in the context of topical units, without their centrality being made explicit. What *Threshold Concepts in Women's and Gender Studies: Ways of Seeing, Thinking, and Knowing* does is not "cover" material but rather "uncover" the key threshold concepts and ways of thinking that students need in order to develop a deep understanding and to approach the material like feminist scholars do, across the disciplines. The advantage of this approach is that rather than the "one-shot definition" that characterizes most texts, students continually learn and relearn how the threshold concept is illustrated across multiple contexts, thus reinforcing their understanding in more substantive ways. Further, foregrounding the "learning roadblocks" that many students encounter as part of the learning process helps circumvent and move more quickly past those misconceptions that keep students from progressing in their understanding of Women's and Gender Studies.

In *Threshold Concepts in Women's and Gender Studies*, we make the assumption that ways of thinking and doing Women's and Gender Studies must be made transparent to students, and that learning will be done most effectively if students understand the course goals, the pedagogical approach, and the potential roadblocks to understanding. We contend that the work happening on the part of the instructor and the work happening by students should not be "parallel tracks" that each negotiates independently, but part of the teaching and learning conversation itself, happening in and about the content, as part of the work of the classroom.

Features

Threshold Concepts in Women's and Gender Studies is organized strategically and conceptually in a reverse pyramid structure. That is, each threshold concept is introduced at a broad level as the key idea of the chapter, while subsequent chapter components add layers of depth and specificity. Each chapter contains the following elements:

- *Opening Illustration*: The opening illustration engages readers in the topic—typically these are drawn from historical, cultural, biological, or current events topics.
- *A Feminist Stance*: We use the framing concept of a "feminist stance" (Crawley, et al.) to help students continue to understand the nature and strategies of a feminist approach with each chapter they read.
- *Definition of the Threshold Concept*: Each chapter focuses on one of four threshold concepts. The chapter opens with a definition of the threshold concept, drawing from established and relevant research across interdisciplinary fields of study.
- *Framing Definitions and Related Concepts*: More specificity is offered by related concepts, or other explanatory terminology by scholars in the field that help students see how the threshold concept is supported and illustrated by related terms.
- *Learning Roadblocks*: Once students have an initial grasp of the concept and its related terms, the chapter introduces common "learning roadblocks" or misconceptions that many students encounter which prevent a full grasp of the idea. These misconceptions are directly addressed along with tools that can serve as a "check for understanding" so students are able to understand not only why these learning roadblocks crop up but also where their own learning is in relation to the roadblocks. The goal of this feature is to help

students identify common misunderstandings that prevent them from "crossing the threshold."

- *Anchoring Topic Discussion*: To further develop students' understanding of the key idea, each chapter includes a discussion about a group of three anchoring topics (work and family; language, images, and symbols; and bodies). Selected issues within the anchoring topics are discussed through the prism of the particular threshold concept, and then returned to with each chapter so that students will develop a multifaceted, nuanced, and complex understanding of the cluster of related issues within the anchoring topics.

- *Case Study*: The case study offers an in-depth, and analytical perspective on one key issue that should crystallize students' understanding of the concept. Case studies have been selected based on relevance to the threshold concept, and to represent a broad range of interdisciplinary issues.

- *Evaluating Prior Knowledge Activities*: As Ambrose and colleagues have observed, students' prior knowledge (particularly common-sense understandings or everyday use of discipline-specific terms) has a strong impact on how students absorb new knowledge. Activities that ask students to evaluate prior knowledge, to monitor their progress, and to develop a metacognitive understanding of their knowledge building stem from this learning principle.

- *Application Exercises*: Gender and women's studies classrooms typically emphasize several key related values focused on participatory learning: validation of personal experience, activism, reflexivity, action orientation, and local–global connections (see Crawley et al., 2008; Stake and Hoffman, 2000; Markowitz, 2005; Maher, 1987a; Shrewsbury, 1993). This praxis orientation (see Blake and Ooten, 2008) is reflected in application exercises for each chapter in which students are invited to connect disciplinary and interdisciplinary knowledge with lived experience.

- *Discussion Questions*: Consistent with the signature feminist pedagogies of Women's and Gender Studies classrooms that focus on collaboration, interconnectedness, and creating a community of learners (see Hassel and Nelson, 2012; Chick and Hassel, 2009), this book adheres to the convention of providing discussion questions for each chapter.

• *Writing Prompts*: The text includes writing activities that encourage students to process, reflect on, and integrate the course material.

• *Suggested Readings and Bibliography*: Each chapter includes a list of suggested readings. The bibliography for the chapter is combined with suggested readings. Because the text is intended to serve as a critical introduction to key concepts and not as a reader, we provide suggested, relevant readings that instructors can use to support and develop students' learning. In this way, we imagine the book to be part of a customized course in which the instructor can structure the curriculum around key ideas, then provide a deeper learning experience for students by adding primary documents, classic essays, or online texts to the course that reflect the instructor's specific learning goals and area of expertise.

Goals of the Book

As coauthors, our goals for this book have been to provide a text that reflects what we have learned about student learning needs in Women's and Gender Studies throughout our collective years of teaching in the field as well as current thinking in the field and in higher education more broadly about what it means to learn within a discipline or interdisciplinary area. The organization of the text around threshold concepts is intended to reflect what Lendol Calder calls an "uncoverage" model, one in which students learn to think, see, and know like feminist scholars rather than absorb a body of knowledge to be "covered."

As a result, our intent is to help students learn those ways of knowing and then to be able to apply them to new subjects, in the way that feminist scholars do. We have tried to reflect in the text some of our shared values as teachers and writers. We have aimed to reflect an up-to-date sensibility both in including recent data and research studies as well as current phenomena. Our tone emphasizes that arguments about sex and gender (and any number of other issues within feminist scholarship and activism) are unresolved, ongoing, and controversial, and the text contextualizes a feminist perspective by explaining what that perspective stands in contrast to.

While we treat each of the four threshold concepts in a separate chapter, which in one sense implies their separability and separateness, they are of course interconnected, and we strive to make those connections explicit within each chapter. In some instances this means returning to the same topic across chapters and highlighting different elements of it. For example, though feminist praxis is its own separate chapter, we have identified the ways that discussions of "problems" within Women's and Gender Studies can be responded to with action or different ways of thinking. Similarly, though intersectionality has its own chapter, we have attempted to incorporate an intersectional perspective and intersectional analysis *throughout* the book, addressing the interrelatedness of systems of privilege and oppression as part of an intersectional examination both across and within topics and themes.

Logistics of Using the Text

While individual programs and pedagogical approaches may vary, the threshold concepts we have identified are central to the content- and skills-based learning outcomes of a large number of Women's and Gender Studies programs nationally (see Levin and Berger and Radeloff). As such, we believe that using a text like ours can be helpful in making those programmatic learning outcomes explicit, and can support the assessment plans of programs and departments.

Logistically, one way to use this book in an introductory WGS course would be to assign all five chapters in succession over the first half of the semester before moving on to a varying number of topics (drawn from our anchoring topics or others of particular interest to the instructor) that would be spread out over the remainder of the semester. In this scenario, all of the threshold concepts would be revisited in the context of each topic.

A different approach to using this book in an introductory WGS course would be to spread the assignment and reading of the five chapters across the course of the entire semester, using one or more topics in relation to each threshold concept. This approach would allow for in-depth time with each individual threshold concept before moving on to the next.

Instructors can find more materials to support their work in the classroom using this text at the companion website (www.routledge.com/cw/launius). Materials available online include the following:

- sample syllabi
- additional suggested readings
- full text journal articles for use with the text

Works Cited

Ambrose, Susan, et al. *How Learning Works: Seven Research-Based Principles for Smart Teaching*. San Francisco, CA: Jossey-Bass, 2010. Print.

Berger, Michelle Tracey, and Cheryl Radeloff. *Transforming Scholarship: Why Women's and Gender Studies Students Are Changing Themselves and the World*. New York: Routledge, 2011. Print.

Blake, Holly, and Melissa Ooten. "Bridging the Divide: Connecting Feminist Histories and Activism in the Classroom." *Radical History Review*. 102 (2008): 63–72. Web.

Calder, Lendol. "Uncoverage: Toward a Signature Pedagogy for the History Survey." *Journal of American History*. 92.4 (March 2006): 1358–1371. Web.

Chick, Nancy, and Holly Hassel. "Don't Hate Me Because I'm Virtual: Feminist Pedagogy in the Online Classroom." *Feminist Teacher*. 19.3 (2009): 195–215. Print.

Cousin, Glynis. "An Introduction to Threshold Concepts." *Planet*. 17 (2006). Web.

Crawley, Sara, et al. "Introduction: Feminist Pedagogies in Action: Teaching Beyond Disciplines." *Feminist Teacher*. 19.1 (2008): 1–12. Web.

Hassel, Holly, and Nerissa Nelson. "A Signature Feminist Pedagogy: Connection and Transformation in Women's Studies." In *Exploring More Signature Pedagogies*. Eds. Nancy L. Chick, Regan Gurung, and Aeron Haynie. Sterling, VA: Stylus P, 2012. 143–155. Print.

Levin, Amy. "Questions for a New Century: Women's Studies and Integrative Learning." *National Women's Studies Association*. NWSA. 2007. Web. 17 May 2012.

Maher, Frances. "Inquiry Teaching and Feminist Pedagogy." *Social Education*. 51.3 (1987): 186–192. Print.

Markowitz, Linda. "Unmasking Moral Dichotomies: Can Feminist Pedagogy Overcome Student Resistance?" *Gender and Education*. 17.1 (2005): 39–55. Print.

Meyer, Jan, and Ray Land. "Threshold Concepts and Troublesome Knowledge: Linkages to Ways of Thinking and Practising within the Disciplines." *Enhancing Teaching-Learning Environments in Undergraduate Courses*. ETL Project. Occasional Report 4, May 2003. Web.

Shrewsbury, Carolyn. "What Is Feminist Pedagogy?" *Women's Studies Quarterly*. 3 (1993): 8–16. Print.

Stake, Jayne, and Frances Hoffman. "Putting Feminist Pedagogy to the Test." *Psychology of Women Quarterly*. 24 (2000): 30–38. Print.

ACKNOWLEDGEMENTS

We owe a deep debt of gratitude to our faculty colleagues in the University of Wisconsin System Women's Studies Consortium. This project emerged from conversations among our fellow Women's and Gender Studies teachers throughout the state of Wisconsin over several years. Their expertise, critical insights, years of teaching experience, and generosity of time and spirit shaped this project from start to finish.

In particular, we thank Helen Klebesadel, director of the Women's Studies Consortium for her tireless support and advocacy for this book; former UW System Gender and Women's Studies Librarian Phyllis Holman Weisbard offered research support in the early stages of the project, and we thank both Phyllis and JoAnne Lehman, editor of *Feminist Collections* for suggesting that we write a review of introductory WGS textbook for *Feminist Collections: A Quarterly of Women's Studies Resources*, published out of the UW System Office of the Women's Studies Librarian. We especially thank JoAnne Lehman for believing in the work and making publication possible.

We are also thankful to the UW System Office of Professional and Instructional Development for a conference mini-grant in 2011 that supported bringing together Women's and Gender Studies instructors to discuss threshold concepts in the field.

Christie would like to acknowledge the support of the University of Wisconsin Oshkosh Faculty Development Program, which funded her small grant proposal. Holly is grateful to the University of Wisconsin–Marathon County which awarded her a Summer Research Grant to complete work on this project, as well as to the UW Colleges Women's Studies Program that has supported her work on threshold concepts in Women's and Gender Studies in material and immaterial ways. Thanks especially to Susan Rensing who helped us work through some of the initial organizational challenges of the text and provided many helpful suggestions along the way. And a thanks to our reviewers:

Courtney Jarrett	Ball State University
Beth Sertell	Ohio University
Daniel Humphrey	Texas A&M University
Jennifer Smith	Pacific Lutheran University
Tanya Kennedy	University of Maine
JoAnna Wall	University of Oklahoma
Shawn Maurer	College of Holy Cross
Danielle DeMuth	Grand Valley State
Desirée Henderson	University of Texas, Arlington
Beatrix Brockman	Austin Peay State University
Marta S. McClintock-Comeaux	California University of Pennsylvania
Lynne Bruckner	Chatham University
Angela Fitzpatrick	Coastal Carolina University

Christie Launius and Holly Hassel

1
INTRODUCTION

All I want is education, and I am afraid of no one.

Malala Yousafzai

Figure 1.1 Anat Ronen, www.anatronen.com

Why "Ways of Seeing, Thinking, and Knowing"?

Women's and Gender Studies (WGS) courses are a common feature on a large number of college and university campuses, with over 700 programs in the United States alone. Many students take an introductory

WGS course as a part of their general education requirements, whereas others wind up in our classrooms as a result of word-of-mouth advertising from peers and roommates. A smaller number of students eagerly seek out WGS courses when they get to college after encountering Women's and Gender Studies in their high school curriculum.

In their book *Transforming Scholarship: Why Women's and Gender Studies Students Are Changing Themselves and the World*, Michele Tracy Berger and Cheryl Radeloff state that "students pursuing questions in women's and gender studies are part of an emerging vanguard of knowledge producers in the US and globally" (5). This is to say, WGS is an exciting, vibrant, and growing field. This textbook aims to introduce you to the ways of seeing, thinking, and knowing that characterize the field and are valued by its practitioners. These ways of seeing, thinking, and knowing can then be used throughout your academic study, not just in WGS courses. More fundamentally, these ways of seeing, thinking, and knowing can be (and perhaps should be) taken out of the classroom and into the world. In fact, the bridging of the divide between academia and the so-called real world is a big part of what Women's and Gender Studies is all about.

The image at the beginning of this chapter (see Figure 1.1) emphasizes this real-world engagement. The words and image of Malala Yousafzai, a young Pakistani woman, are highlighted because her struggle—to gain access to education for girls in a Pakistani area in which the Taliban has prohibited it—illustrates how feminist ways of seeing, thinking, and knowing are actualized. The image, invoking the historically significant "Rosie the Riveter" pose that has come to symbolize women's entrance into the workforce in the mid-20th century, shows the historical roots of feminist movement and how they continue to influence women's **activism** worldwide.

Using This Book

As you approach this text, we want to direct your attention to the ways that we have organized it in order to provide an introduction to the ways of seeing, thinking, and knowing in Women's and Gender Studies. Each chapter is structured in purposeful ways in order to introduce you to the definitions of the **threshold concept** and to offer grounding examples that will deepen your understanding:

- the opening illustration in each chapter invites you to consider how the concept is relevant to day-to-day life, either current events, popular culture, historical moments, or other spaces.
- we have indicated in each chapter how the concept suggests a "feminist stance," or a way of looking at the world.
- threshold concepts are defined, as are related or supporting concepts from research, theory, or scholarship that are critical to understanding the ideas in the chapter.
- each chapter includes examples of "learning roadblocks," or the kinds of barriers to fully understanding the threshold concept that students typically encounter. We've drawn from our many years of teaching introductory Women's and Gender Studies courses as well as conversations with colleagues to identify these roadblocks as well as explain why they are common misconceptions, and how students can move past them.
- in order to illustrate in a fuller way how the threshold concept operates in interdisciplinary forms, each of the concepts is discussed through the lens of "anchoring topics," or key ideas that will root the concept within three overlapping and related areas of inquiry within Women's and Gender Studies: work and family; language, images, and symbols, and gendered bodies. As you engage with each of the chapters, you'll develop not only a new understanding of the threshold concept in that chapter, but an increasingly deepening sense of how each of the anchoring topics is "inflected" by the concepts.
- each chapter contains a case study that, like the opening illustration, is intended to bring the threshold concept to life for readers and to see how it can be understood through specific cultural, historical, or other phenomena.
- finally, at the end of the chapter, you'll find exercises and other ways to test your understanding of the chapter material, to engage in conversation with classmates, to write about the topic, and to apply what you've learned to other contexts.

We hope that this organizational structure will create multiple ways of "trying on" feminist ways of seeing, thinking, and knowing in academic and nonacademic spaces.

Feminism, Stereotypes, and Misconceptions

First and foremost, in order to understand terms like "feminist stance" and the idea that there are **feminist** ways of seeing, thinking, and knowing, some definitions of **feminism** are in order. As a term, feminism has a history; according to Estelle Freedman, it was "first coined in France in the 1880s as *feminisme*," (3) and made its way to the United States by the first decade of the 20th century. It was not used widely in the United States until the 1960s, however. In *No Turning Back: The History of Feminism and the Future of Women*, Freedman offers a four-part definition of feminism: "Feminism is a belief that women and men are inherently of equal worth. Because most societies privilege men as a group, social movements are necessary to achieve equality between women and men, with the understanding that gender always intersects with other social hierarchies" (7). bell hooks offers a succinct definition of feminism as "the struggle to end sexist oppression" (26). She goes on to argue that understanding and defining feminism in this way "directs our attention to systems of domination and the inter-relatedness of **sex**, race, and class oppression" (31). She concludes, "The foundation of future feminist struggle must be solidly based on a recognition of the need to eradicate the underlying cultural basis and causes of **sexism** and other forms of group oppression" (31). Given these definitions, a feminist, then, is quite simply someone who advocates feminism. Each of the four threshold concepts that this book is structured around are implicit, if not explicit, in both Freedman's and hooks's definitions: the social construction of **gender**, the concepts of **privilege** and **oppression, intersectionality**, and **praxis**.

Advocating feminism or being a feminist can take many forms; in this book we emphasize the idea of taking a so-called feminist stance, which is to say, adopting a feminist perspective or way of looking at the world. As Crawley and colleagues assert,

> Although feminism is, in substance, always attentive to power differences that create inequalities, particularly those that create

differential opportunities for women and men (but also those that create racial and ethnic, class-based, or sexuality-based inequalities), feminism is also an epistemological shift away from a history of androcentric bias in the sciences, social sciences, and humanities. As such, it is not just an "area study" (again, not just about "women") but something much deeper: a way of orienting to academic work that is attuned to power relations, both within the academy and within knowledge construction itself.

(2)

We will discuss this at more length in the section on the history of Women's and Gender Studies as an academic field.

It also seems important to address here at the outset any lingering misconceptions about feminism and feminists. Many stereotypes and misconceptions about feminism, feminists, and the field of Women's and Gender Studies circulate in our culture. These stereotypes and misconceptions pop up in the right-wing blogosphere and so-called lad mags like *Maxim*, but also in magazines like *Time* and *Newsweek*, in Hollywood movies and television shows, and in everyday conversations. Most students taking this course have probably heard quite a few of them. If you're curious about whether your friends, family, coworkers, and others believe those stereotypes and misconceptions, try this exercise: make an announcement on the social media platform of your choice that you're taking this class, and see what sorts of responses are made and what sorts of conversations develop. Chances are, people will supply some of the following (and maybe come up with different ones as well):

- *"Feminism is dead."* This misconception is invoked as a way to try to derail or shut down a discussion of gender inequality, a way to dismiss someone's critique by saying that we no longer need feminism because equality has already been achieved. The most charitable read on this stereotype is that people look at the real gains made by feminism and mistakenly assume that the need for feminism has passed. In this scenario, the person claiming that equality has already been achieved is likely experiencing the world from a position of relative privilege. The misconception doesn't just get perpetuated on an individual level, however; it is a frequent headline in the news media. In response to *Time*'s cover story in 1998 declaring feminism dead, feminist writer Erica Jong noted that "there have been no less than 119 articles in the magazine sticking pins in feminism during the last 25 years." All of this raises the question, as Jessica Valenti puts it, "if feminism is dead, then why do people have to keep on trying to kill it?" (11)

- *Feminists are ugly, hairy, braless, don't wear makeup, etc. Emphasis on the ugly.* A feature called "Cure a Feminist," which appeared in the November 2003 issue of *Maxim*, does a good job of illustrating this stereotype.[1] It features four images of the same woman wearing different clothing and displaying different body language that purport to show the transformation from feminist to "actual girl." The "feminist" is wearing baggy jeans and a so-called wifebeater tank top with no bra. Her hair is messy, and her arm is raised to reveal a hairy armpit. She also has a cigarette dangling from her mouth, and she is standing with legs apart, with one hand hooked into the pocket of her jeans. By the end of her transformation, she is wearing nothing but a lacy bra and panties with high heels, standing with one hip jutted out and her hand tugging her underwear down. Her hair is styled and she is wearing makeup. The intent of this stereotype is fairly simplistic and transparent, but nonetheless hard to shake. As Jessica Valenti puts it, "The easiest way to keep women—especially young women—away from feminism is to threaten them with the ugly stick. It's also the easiest way to dismiss someone and her opinions" (8–9).

- *Feminists hate men.* The *Maxim* piece hits this stereotype, too. The implication here is that feminism is a hate-filled vendetta against individual men. The thought bubble coming out of the so-called feminist's mouth says, "There'd be no more wars if all penises were cut off! Argh!" This misconception is a strategy to dismiss and mischaracterize feminism and feminists, by individualizing feminist concerns and seeing feminism as a battle of the sexes, rather than a structural analysis of systems of privilege and inequality. A more accurate characterization recognizes that feminism is interested in critiquing and combating sexism and **patriarchy**, not hating or bashing individual men.

- *Only women can be feminists.* It is clear, in the *Maxim* feature and elsewhere, that the default assumption is that only women would *want* to be feminists, given that feminists hate men, and that only women stand to gain from feminism. This view is increasingly being challenged, not only because a growing number of men are committed to being strong feminist **allies** to the women in their lives, but also because men increasingly see the ways in which they are harmed by adhering to traditional masculine norms. These men are stepping outside of the so-called man box and are modeling feminist forms of **masculinity**.

- *Feminists are lesbians (or male feminists are gay).* This misconceptions often circulates as a dissuasion strategy that is sometimes referred to as "lesbian-baiting" or "gay-baiting," that is, as a way of capitalizing on social stigma within some communities to scare women and men away from openly identifying as feminist or even supporting key principles of gender equity. As philosopher Sue Cataldi has argued, "The use of this word is a scare tactic. It is intended to frighten people away from affiliating with or associating with feminism" (80). By associating feminist movement with stigmatized groups, antifeminist activists succeed in maintaining the current power structure.

- *Feminists are making a big deal out of nothing.* In addition to harnessing the social power of **homophobia** to discredit **feminist action** and theory, such stereotypes serve the purpose of reinforcing traditional gender scripts and sexualities. As Suzanne Pharr explains in "Homophobia as a Weapon of Sexism": "What does a woman have to do to get called a lesbian? Almost anything, sometimes nothing at all, but certainly anything that threatens the status quo, anything that steps out of role, anything that asserts the rights of women, anything that doesn't include submission or subordination" (73). As this text establishes, the need for feminist action to address women's low social status, patriarchal society, and the overall devaluation of women and **femininity** is very clear.

The effect of these stereotypes and misconceptions: many people, particularly young women, are reluctant to identify as feminists. The title of Lisa Hogeland's oft-anthologized essay, originally published in *Ms. Magazine* in 1994, spells it out: "Fear of Feminism: Why Young Women Get the Willies." Hogeland explains, aptly and pointedly, that at least one reason is "The central feminist tenet that **the personal is political** is profoundly threatening to young women who don't want to be called to account. It is far easier to rest in silence, as if silence were neutrality, and as if neutrality were safety" (Hogeland). That is, calling into question current gender arrangements requires girls and women (and boys and men) to actively and consciously challenge the ways that gender inequality persists instead of, as Hogeland states, "hide from feminist issues by not being feminists."

More recently, feminist blogger Julie Zeilinger has jumped into the fray, and the title of her book indicates that what she calls a "P.R.-problem" with feminism is still going on: *A Little F'ed Up: Why Feminism Is Not a Dirty Word* (2012). Both Zeilinger and Jessica Valenti, among many others, bemoan what they call the "I'm not a feminist, but . . ." phenomenon, in which people express feminist ideas and opinions but disavow the label. Their response is to argue that most young people *are* feminists, but, as Zeilinger puts it, "They just don't know it" (79). Or as Valenti titles the first chapter of *Full Frontal Feminism: A Young Woman's Guide to Why Feminism Matters*: "You're a hardcore feminist. I swear" (5). In sum, while both Zeilinger and Valenti grant that the stereotypes and misconceptions about feminism and feminists continue to swirl through our news media and popular culture, and get internalized and perpetuated by many, they clearly believe that, with a dose of corrective information to counter the stereotypes, people can and do see them for what they are, which is an attempt to undermine feminism.

Proof that attitudes about gender equality have changed is abundant, as documented, for example, in the results of this survey by the Pew Research Center, which shows that almost three-quarters of young adults under the age of 30 seek equal partnership marriages (see Figure 1.2).

Stephanie Coontz cites this research as a positive sign of feminist progress, but she follows up by showing that in reality, many couples have a very hard time putting these aspirations into practice. In "Why

Young Adults Favor Dual-Income Marriage

% who prefer a marriage in which husband and wife both have jobs/take care of the house and children

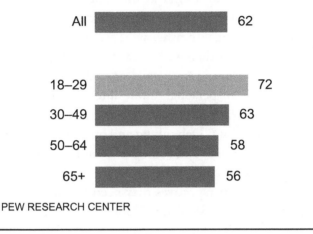

PEW RESEARCH CENTER

Figure 1.2

Source: Pew Research Center survey, conducted Oct 1–21, 2010, N = 2, 691.

Q wording: What kind of marriage do you think is the more satisfying way of life? One where the husband provides for the family and the wife takes care of the house and children, or one where the husband and wife both have jobs and both take care of the house and children.

Gender Equality Stalled," she argues that the "main barriers to further progress toward gender equity no longer lie in people's personal attitudes and relationships. Instead, structural impediments prevent people from acting on their egalitarian values, forcing men and women into personal accommodations and rationalizations that do not reflect their preferences." The structural impediments Coontz is referring to are the gender wage gap, the relative absence of family-friendly workplace policies, and the lack of high-quality affordable and accessible child care. How does this relate back to the stereotypes and misconceptions about feminism and feminists, you ask?

The fact that almost three-quarters of people under 30 aspire to an **egalitarian** marriage shows that the discrediting of feminism and feminist values through the dissemination of stereotypes has largely not succeeded, at least in terms of the attitudes documented by research. On the other hand, however, the demonization or dismissal of feminism *has* succeeded insofar as the couples who try and fail to enact their egalitarian values tend to think of their failure in personal, rather than political, terms. In other words, they think that the problem lies with them rather than with broader, structural factors outside of their immediate control. And most crucially, they are less likely to turn those feelings of personal failure into a recognition that this is a political issue that could be and is being addressed by feminists and feminist organizations. Debunking and offering rebuttals to those stereotypes about feminism and feminists is not just (or only) about countering myth with reality, then, but about helping to give people the necessary tools and perspectives they need to change the world in ways that allow them to, as Stephanie Coontz puts it, "put their gender values into practice." All of this illustrates why the feminist mantra of the second wave, "The personal is political," resonates across issues and experience.

Feminist ways of seeing, thinking, and knowing provide tools for the critical analysis of stereotypes about feminism and feminists. Calling yourself a feminist (or advocating feminism, as bell hooks puts it) may or may not be the outcome of trying on these ways of seeing, thinking, and knowing, and in any case, that's not the point. The point is to clear the space for everyone to consider feminism on its own terms, free from bias and distortion.

The History of Feminist Movement

The awareness of gendered inequality and women's (and male allies') efforts to eliminate inequality has a long history. However, in terms of organized activism on the part of women's groups in the United States to address long-standing oppressions such as a lack of civil rights, access to higher education and the professions, inequitable treatment by the legal system, and a lack of social and cultural status, the history is more recent.

It should be noted that the term most commonly used to describe feminist activism in the United States is **waves**, with chronological groupings of the first wave, beginning in the mid-19th century and progressing through the early 20th century; the second wave, starting in the mid-1960s; and the third wave, starting in the early 1990s. However, this is largely an organizational convenience and may not only overshadow the ongoing, active efforts on the part of many activists to challenge patriarchal values, norms, and practices, but also overemphasize the contributions of white and middle-class feminists. In what follows we will both acknowledge the "waves" narrative while simultaneously complicating it.

The first wave of feminism is widely considered to have its origins in the activist efforts of a group of early feminists: Lucretia Mott and Elizabeth Cady Stanton attempted to attend the World Anti-Slavery Convention in London in 1840 and were barred from participating because of their sex. In 1848, Mott and Stanton joined Martha Wright, Mary Ann McClintock, and Jane Hunt in organizing a two-day meeting of women to be held at a church in Seneca Falls, New York. Several hundred people attended, and another 100 (68 women and 32 men) signed the document drafted by Stanton, "Declaration of Sentiments," modeled on the U.S. Declaration of Independence. It included the first formal demand for access to the "elective franchise," or voting rights, for women, and claimed: "The history of mankind is a history of repeated injuries and usurpations on the part of man toward woman, having in direct object the establishment of an absolute tyranny over her. To prove this, let facts be submitted to a candid world." The document not only made demands for property rights and the right to participate civically including voting, but also for recourse in the case of marital abuse and custodial authority over their children in the case of divorce. It also demanded greater participation in the activities of the church and access to educational and professional opportunities.

An issue that feminists and **suffrage** activists dedicated a great deal of attention to was the **Equal Rights Amendment (ERA)**, introduced in 1923 as an effort to cast in policy equal rights for women. However, it took fifty years before the amendment passed both houses of the legislature and ultimately, because it could not win the ratification requirements of 38 states, the amendment failed to be adopted. The text of the amendment reads as follows:

- **Section 1.** Equality of rights under the law shall not be denied or abridged by the United States or by any State on account of sex.
- **Section 2.** The Congress shall have the power to enforce, by appropriate legislation, the provisions of this article.
- **Section 3.** This amendment shall take effect two years after the date of ratification.[2]

Consider that, although many feminist organizations campaigned tirelessly for the passage of the ERA, a strong and vocal minority of women activists, notably Phyllis Schlafly, campaigned against it. They argued that it would eradicate a number of privileges that women enjoyed on the basis of their primary roles as wives and mothers, including entitlement to maintenance (alimony) and child support in the case of divorce and protection from being drafted in times of war.

The first wave of feminism, then, focused largely on gaining rights for women *as citizens* of the United States. It should be noted that this narrative has been challenged by Paula Gunn Allen in her book *The Sacred Hoop*, where she notes that a full 250 years prior to the Seneca Falls convention, Iroquois women held great power and were respected within their communities. She argues that the women-led tribes of the American continent "provided the basis for all the dreams of liberation that characterize the modern world," although they are rarely credited with having done so. This supports some of the critiques that have been made in the past about early feminist movement, focusing primarily on the rights and activism of middle class white women without a clear focus on equivalent civic activism for women of color and working-class women.

Since these early efforts at achieving suffrage—women were granted the right to vote in 1920 when the 19th Amendment was ratified—feminist activism since the late 1960s has focused on an array of issues widely considered to be the "second wave" of feminist activism. Issues during the 1960s and 1970s included: reproductive justice, including not just the ability to prevent conception and terminate unwanted pregnancy but also the freedom from involuntary sterilization; access to prenatal care and breastfeeding support; expanded educational and occupational opportunities; access to other political and civic rights; safety from violence; and elimination of cultural sexism including sexual **objectification**, lower social status, and the socialization of women to meet the needs of men. Strong gains were made in the 1960s and 1970s in particular, during the height of the second wave of feminism, including:

- national, legal access to contraceptive technologies, including the contraceptive pill, which was prohibited by law prior to 1965.
- national, legal access to abortion in the first trimester of pregnancy, with the landmark ruling in *Roe v. Wade* by the Supreme Court in 1973.
- the establishment of women's organizations such as the National Organization for Women (NOW), founded in 1966, largely focused equal opportunity in the workplace.
- advocacy for equal pay. In the 1970s, women made, on average, 52 cents to the average man's dollar; today, that hovers around 80.8% of the male dollar, still short of equality. When breaking these numbers down by race, they are even more troubling: as the Institute for Women's Policy Research documents, the percentages fall to 68.1% for black women and 59.3% for Hispanic women (Institute).
- activism for legislation like the Equal Pay Act (1963), intended to ensure equal wages for all workers, prohibiting discrimination on the basis of sex; the Civil Rights Act (1964), for the protection from harassment on the basis of sex; the Pregnancy Discrimination Act (1978), which protected women from job loss or consequences on the basis of pregnancy.
- prevention of gender-based violence, including establishment of **Take Back the Night** rallies (1976); creation of **Rape Shield Laws** in the 1970s and 1980s on the state level preventing a rape victim's past sexual history from being used as evidence in a rape trial; formation of the National Coalition Against Domestic Violence (1978); and the passage of the **Violence Against Women Act** (1994), which offered coordinated efforts to develop awareness and prevent violence.
- passage of **Title IX**. This part of the Education Amendments of 1972 guarantees equal participation in any educational program or

activity that receives federal financial resources. Although primarily associated with advancing women's equal participation in athletic activities, Title IX also affected women's achievement of postsecondary degrees and pay equity within schools, and protection from any other discrimination taking place within an educational setting ("Fast Facts").

- social advocacy for programs like affordable child care; social safety nets to support poor women; and rape crisis centers and domestic violence shelters for women who have been victims of violence.

A third wave of feminism arose in the early 1990s, sparked by the Supreme Court confirmation hearings of Justice Clarence Thomas. The hearings were marked by accusations that Thomas had sexually harassed Anita Hill when she worked for him at the Department of Education and the Equal Employment Opportunity Commission. The televised hearings riveted and outraged many, as Hill was subjected to harsh and dismissive questioning, and Thomas pushed back against the accusations, calling the hearings a "high-tech lynching." Thomas's remark referenced the nation's shameful history of white mobs lynching African American men for supposed sexual misbehavior, thus casting the hearings in a racial frame. Many others attempted to read the episode primarily using a gender frame, highlighting the ways that Hill's accusations of sexual harassment were belittled and dismissed by both Thomas and the white male senators conducting the hearings. Chapter 4's focus on intersectionality will delve further into the dangers of a single-axis analysis and explore the political and analytical developments of an intersectional approach that is able to analyze incidents such as this one in all its complexity.

Rebecca Walker, daughter of prominent second-wave feminist Alice Walker, penned what became the rallying cry for third-wave feminists. In her essay, "Becoming the Third Wave," Walker sounded the call for a revitalization of feminist activism that in particular was aimed at young women who were literally or metaphorically the daughters of second-wave feminism. Subsequently, feminist movement in the United States has focused on continued efforts for workplace rights for all women, **work–life balance** policies, reduction of violence against women;

equality within **institutions** like religious institutions and the military; resistance to the objectification of women in the media and popular culture; racial justice; and **LGBTQ** rights. We will survey many contemporary feminist activist issues, tactics, and strategies in Chapter 5.

Internationally, feminist activists focus on economic equality for women, equal political representation of women in the legislature and leadership positions, and the overall undervaluing of women's labor. They also focus on preventing forms of patriarchal violence[3] like sex-selective abortion and son preference, **honor killings**, the treatment of women as a form of property, female **infanticide, female genital cutting/ female circumcision, intimate partner violence** and marital rape, sex work and sex trafficking, and pornography. Feminists around the globe use a variety of strategies and tactics in their work on these issues. Sometimes they disagree about the best approach, as in the cases of sex work and pornography, in which some advocate legalization, reform, and regulation by the state, whereas others argue for abolition.

Returning to the second wave of feminism, which arose in the late 1960s, part of that activist work centered on the dearth of scholarly and academic work by and women, as well as the desire for an institutional and educational infrastructure that could support and implement feminist work. Out of these motivations, the field of women's studies emerged.

Women's and Gender Studies as an Academic Field

As a field of academic study, with courses, faculty, and majors and minors, Women's and Gender Studies stretches back over 40 years, with the first women's studies courses and programs created in the late 1960s and early 1970s.

The further away we get from the founding of the field, the harder it is to remember what higher education was like prior to its creation. In their Prologue to *Manifesta: Young Women, Feminism, and the Future*, Jennifer Baumgardner and Amy Richards open with a vignette about what life was like in the United States in 1970 (the year they were born). In the section on higher education, they remind us that in 1970 there were still a small number of colleges and universities that barred women from enrolling, and that women's colleges were still referred to as "girls' schools." They also note that many campuses maintained curfew times for female students who lived in the dorms.

The timing of the field's creation is no coincidence; as mentioned earlier, it came into being in the United States during the second wave of feminism, or the **women's liberation** movement. Indeed, for many years afterward, women's studies was often referred to as the academic arm of the women's movement. Professors and students who identified as feminists began questioning and critiquing many aspects of higher education, including *what* was being taught, *how* it was being taught, and *by whom*. They pointed out that women's experiences and perspectives were for the most part absent in the curriculum, and they also noted the relative absence of women in the ranks of professors and administrators. According to Marilyn J. Boxer, the absence of women's voices and perspectives in academia itself constituted a "hidden curriculum of women's second-class status." She continues, "In this view, courses that ignored women's experiences and perspectives subtly reinforced old ideas about female intellectual deficiencies while also perpetuating women's social, economic, and political marginality" (43). For example, students and professors in English departments began to question why there were so few women authors included in literary anthologies and therefore on course syllabi. Professors' efforts to rectify that situation led to the exploration of broader issues such as canon formation and the role of publishers and critics. During this initial period of field development, the main question was, "Where are the women?"

In creating new courses and undertaking new research projects that focused on women and placed their experiences at the center of inquiry, early practitioners realized that they both wanted and needed to go beyond the boundaries of any single academic discipline. Feminist scholars interested in researching motherhood, for example, wanted not only to explore how motherhood had been represented in literature, but also wanted to look at psychological theories of motherhood, or sociological studies that were focused on interviewing women about their experiences of motherhood. The new courses and scholarship, then, frequently had a multidisciplinary or interdisciplinary approach. This emphasis has endured within the field; for example, the scholarship cited in this textbook comes from the fields of history, psychology, sociology, literary studies, public health, and media studies, to name a few. Today, Women's and Gender Studies programs have become the academic home of the courses and scholarship that go beyond the boundaries of a single discipline. In addition, disciplinary courses and scholarship with a feminist focus continue to thrive; the difference in these courses is that they are more focused on the conventions and conversations that practitioners of a single field are interested in.

Over the last four decades, women's studies has grown not just in terms of its numbers and reach across campuses, but also in terms of how it defines and understands its focus and objects of inquiry. For example, while the field first started as "women's studies," the forms of academic inquiry about gender, and new theories, paradigms, and empirical evidence, have resulted in a field of study more accurately titled "women's and gender studies," or "gender, sexuality, and women's studies," or sometimes more pointedly, "feminist studies." Titles of programs or departments or courses often reflect the interests and emphases of particular institutions or faculty in postsecondary education.

If the initial question of the field was "Where are the women?", by the 1980s that question had shifted to "Which women?" Feminist historian Estelle Freedman explains the shift this way: "I believe that we must question both the assumption that the term *man* includes woman as well as the assumption that the term *woman* represents the diversity of female experience" (8). It was during this period that one of the threshold concepts of this book, intersectionality, began to be developed by women of color who correctly noted the limitations of scholarship that did not incorporate considerations of difference. This concept is the focus of Chapter 4.

The name changes that included the terms gender and sexuality reflect the fact that today, research and teaching are often not exclusively focused on women, but also on men and masculinity, and even further, to the questioning of gender as a binary construct. Thus, for example, we are seeing the emergence of courses on **trans*** issues and identities. At the same time, many programs have incorporated content and degree programs in LGBTQ Studies and the study of sexuality more generally. Finally, the field has also become increasingly global and comparative in focus. The National Women's Studies Association notes that the field draws on the "conceptual claims and theoretical practices of transnationalism, which focus on cultures, structures, and relationships that are formed as a result of the flows of people and resources across geopolitical borders."

Today, the glass is simultaneously half-full and half-empty. On the one hand, huge strides have been made in terms of the numbers of colleges and universities offering courses, minors, and majors in WGS; in terms of the broader integration of gender issues across the curriculum; and in terms of the numbers of women who are professors and administrators. Many students find that they are introduced to issues of gender and sexuality in any number of college courses, only some of which are explicitly designated as Women's and Gender Studies courses. On the other hand, however, women are still overrepresented among the ranks of temporary, part-time, and adjunct faculty, and are woefully underrepresented in the science, technology, engineering, and mathematics (STEM) fields. According to the White House Office of Science and Technology Policy, for example, women today currently earn 41% of PhDs in STEM fields, but make up only 28% of tenure-track faculty in those fields.

Some disciplines more than others have been slow to integrate content on women, gender, and feminism into their curricula; philosophy is a good example. Not coincidentally, philosophy also has some of the lowest numbers of female faculty members. A *Chronicle of Higher Education* story explains that women earned "31 percent of bachelor's degrees in philosophy in 2006–7, compared with 41 percent in history, 45 percent in mathematics, 60 percent in biology, and 69 percent in English, to name several other fields. Moreover, women earned just 27 percent of philosophy doctorates in 2006, and they currently make up only 21 percent of professional philosophers" (Penaluna). Some theories about these low numbers include explanations ranging from the content itself—the canon of philosophy is almost exclusively made up of male philosophers, or as Penaluna argues, "the canon is sexist and there is little being done about it." Other theories include the low regard for feminist philosophy, overt sexism or misogyny within the field of academic philosophy, and historical associations between men/masculinity and analysis and logic, the hallmarks of academic philosophy.

The progress that has been made in academic and nonacademic settings is in some ways a double-edged sword. As Howe explains, "In short, students—and some younger faculty as well—may have two different kinds of experiences today: A majority may still be where we were thirty years ago, unknowingly in a male-centered curriculum; a minority may think that women have always been a part of the curriculum" (29). This text aims to introduce you to the many important achievements of feminist work—as well as draw attention to how a feminist stance or lens can make visible the additional work to be done to gain full social equality for all.

Case Study: The Bechdel Test

Feminist critics apply the lens of gender to a variety of settings. The Bechdel test is one such example. In a 1985 comic strip, "Dykes to Watch Out For," Allison Bechdel introduced this method for assessing gender bias in narratives: fiction, film, TV shows—any text that offers a storyline. Visit the Bechdel test website to see how your favorite (or least favorite) films pass or fail this test of gender and sexism in media.[4] Anita Sarkeesian discusses "The Oscars and the Bechdel Test" on her website, Feminist Frequency.[5] Keep this approach in mind as you read about gender and the Oscars in Chapter 2.

End of Chapter Elements

Application Exercises

1. Select one of the following feminist issues discussed in this chapter and do some Internet research. What is the current status of that issue? What policy or legislative efforts are currently at work in that issue? How do you see the issue in your own day-to-day life?
   - Access to **contraception**
   - Access to safe, legal abortion
   - Access to breastfeeding support and space
   - Social support services including Temporary Assistance for Needy Families or Supplemental Nutrition Assistance Program funding
   - Affordable child care
   - LGBTQ rights

- Trans* issues
- Media and popular culture images of women (and men)
- Working conditions including recourse in the case of unequal pay, pregnancy discrimination, and sexual harassment
- Violence against women
- Women in **electoral politics**

2. Review the core principles of the ERA described in this chapter. What arguments can you see being made in favor of the ERA? What arguments do you imagine being made against it? Which do you see as more persuasive, and why?

3. To further investigate the Bechdel test, select two or three of your favorite films. Watch them again with a specific and careful eye toward dialogue, action, and interaction between characters. Do they "pass" the Bechdel test? What would the films look like if they did? How would they look different, and what would need to be added or changed in order to increase the representation and depth of the women characters in it?

4. View the 2004 film *Iron-Jawed Angels*, an account of the suffrage movement. Write out responses in which you explore the following questions: Why did 19th-century activists focus so heavily on women's right to vote? In what ways is it a significant form of civic participation? What other issues might have been neglected because of a focus on suffrage, and why?

Skills Assessment/Check for Understanding

1. Write a short response in which you summarize the key issues that feminist activism has focused on over the course of the last two centuries.

2. Consider your own educational experiences. To what degree has the study of gender and the inclusion of women been (a) made visible? (b) part of the curriculum? (c) taken for granted? That is, in history courses, were you taught about women's roles and contributions, or did your studies focus primarily on military and political history? In literature courses, did you read work by women writers? Are there other examples of gender equity or inequity that stand out to you from your own academic experiences? In your answers, consider

your experiences in elementary school, middle school, high school, and college.

Discussion Questions

1. Feminist bell hooks argues in *Feminism Is for Everybody* that feminists in developed countries have oversimplified feminist thinking, charging that "linking circumcision with life-threatening eating disorders (which are the direct consequence of a culture imposing thinness as a beauty ideal) or any life-threatening cosmetic surgery would emphasize the sexism, the misogyny, underlying these practices globally mirror the sexism here in this country" (47). That is, bell hooks asks us to consider the relationship between various forms of social control over women's bodies and whether one is more horrific than another (and if not, whose interests are served by ranking them so). Do these parallels ring true to you? Why or why not?

2. Which of the stereotypes and misconceptions about feminism and feminists discussed in this chapter have you encountered before? Where and in what context?

Writing Prompts

1. *Reflection*: When people talk about feminism as "political," they often mean very different things. Critics of feminism and Women's and Gender Studies argue that it's focused on electoral politics and partisan issues (like abortion or pay equity) and therefore is not academic. Proponents use "political" to mean that it is rooted in concepts of power. Which meaning resonates the most with you? What examples can you think of to illustrate it?

2. Trace your understanding of feminism and feminists, based on your earliest exposure to the term or ideas to any new understanding you have gained reading this chapter and any other texts used for your course. Identify any learning goals you have for the rest of the course, and lingering questions or points of concern that you have about your experience in a Women's and Gender Studies course.

3. *Research project*: Select a single issue or focus of feminist movement over the last two centuries. In a formal academic paper, trace how

that issue has evolved in a specific place and what progress has been made. Identify areas for future work.

Notes

1 www.about-face.org/maxim-magazine-considers-feminism-a-disease-to-be-cured/
2 http://en.wikipedia.org/wiki/Equal_Rights_Amendment—cite_note-2
3 bell hooks defines "patriarchal violence" in her book *Feminism Is for Everybody* this way: "Patriarchal violence in the home is based on the belief that it is acceptable for a more powerful individual to control others through various forms of coercive force. This expanded definition of domestic violence includes male violence against women, same-sex violence, and adult violence against children. The term 'patriarchal violence' is useful because unlike the more acceptable phrase 'domestic violence' it continually reminds the listener that violence in the home is connected to sexism and sexist thinking, to male domination. For too long the term domestic violence has been used as a 'soft' term which suggests it emerges in an intimate context that is private and somehow less threatening, less brutal, than the violence that takes place outside the home. This is not so, since more women are beaten and murdered in the home than on the outside. Also most people tend to see domestic violence between adults as separate and distinct from violence against children when it is not. Often children suffer abuse as they attempt to protect a mother who is being attacked by a male companion or husband, or they are emotionally damaged by witnessing violence and abuse."
4 http://bechdeltest.com/
5 www.youtube.com/watch?v=bLF6sAAMb4s

Works Cited and Suggested Readings

Allen, Paula Gunn. *The Sacred Hoop.* Boston: Beacon P, 1986. Print.

Baumgardner, Jennifer, and Amy Richards. *Manifesta: Young Women, Feminism, and the Future.* New York: Farrar, Strauss, and Giroux, 2000. Print.

Berger, Michele Tracy, and Cheryl Radeloff. *Transforming Scholarship: Why Women's and Gender Studies Students are Changing Themselves and the World.* New York: Routledge, 2011. Print.

Boxer, Marilyn J. "Women's Studies as Women's History." *Women's Studies Quarterly.* 30 (2002): 42–51. Print.

Cataldi, Sue. "Reflections on Male-Bashing." *NWSA Journal.* 7.2 (1995): 76–85. Web.

Coontz, Stephanie. "Why Gender Equality Stalled." *New York Times.* 16 February 2013. Web.

Crawley, Sara, et al. "Introduction: Feminist Pedagogies in Action: Teaching Beyond-Disciplines." *Feminist Teacher.* 19.1 (2008): 1–12. Web.

Dicker, Rory. *A Brief History of U.S. Feminisms.* Berkeley, CA: Seal P, 2008. Print.

"Domestic Violence Prevention: A History of Milestones and Achievements." VAWNet.org. National Online Resources Center on Violence Against Women. 2011. Web.

"Fast Facts: Title IX." National Center for Education Statistics. U.S. Department of Education. 2014. Web.

Freedman, Estelle. *No Turning Back: The History of Feminism and the Future of Women.* New York: Ballantine Books, 2002. Print.

———. *The Essential Feminist Reader.* New York: Modern Library, 2007. Print.

Hogeland, Lisa. "Fear of Feminism: Why Young Women Get the Willies." *Ms. Magazine.* 1 December 1994. Web.

hooks, bell. *Feminist Theory from Margin to Center.* Boston: South End P, 1984. Print.

———. *Feminism Is for Everybody: Passionate Politics.* Cambridge, MA: South End P, 2000. Print.

Howe, Florence. "Still Changing Academe after All These Years." *Women's Studies Quarterly.* 30 (2002): 27–31. Print.

Institute for Women's Policy Research. "Fact Sheet: The Gender Wage Gap, 2013: Differences by Race and Ethnicity No Growth in Real Wages for Women." IWPR#C413. March 2014. Web.

Iron-Jawed Angels. Dir. Katja van Garnier. Perf. Hilary Swank, Margo Martindale, Anjelica Huston, Frances O'Connor, Vera Farmiga, and Lois Smith. HBO, 2004. Film.

Jong, Erica. "Ally McBeal and Time Magazine Can't Keep the Good Women Down." *New York Observer.* 13 July 1998. Web.

Kennedy, Elizabeth Lapovsky, and Agatha Beins, eds. *Women's Studies for the Future.* New Brunswick, NJ: Rutgers UP, 2005. Print.

Moran, Caitlin. *How to Be a Woman.* New York: HarperCollins, 2012. Print.

National Women's Studies Association. 23 April 2014 Web.

Orr, Catherine, Ann Braithwaite, and Diane Lichtenstein, eds. *Rethinking Women's and Gender Studies.* New York: Routledge, 2011. Print.

Penaluna, Regan. "Wanted: Female Philosophers, in the Classroom and in the Canon." *The Chronicle of Higher Education.* 11 October 2009. Web.

Pharr, Suzanne. "Homophobia as a Weapon of Sexism." *Women's Voices, Feminist Visions: Classic and Contemporary Readings.* Boston: McGraw-Hill, 2007. Print. 71–74.

"The Women's Rights Movement, 1848–1920." *History, Art, and Archives. The United States House of Representatives.* Web.

Valenti, Jessica. *Full Frontal Feminism: A Young Woman's Guide to Why Feminism Matters.* Berkeley, CA: Seal P, 2007. Print.

Walker, Rebecca. "Becoming the Third Wave." *Ms. Magazine.* 2.4 (January 1992): 39–41. Print.

Wiegman, Robyn, ed. *Women's Studies on its Own: A Next Wave Reader on Institutional Change.* Durham, NC: Duke UP, 2002. Print.

Zeilinger, Julie. *A Little F'd Up: Why Feminism Is Not a Dirty Word.* Berkeley, CA: Seal Press, 2012. Print.

2

THE SOCIAL CONSTRUCTION
OF GENDER

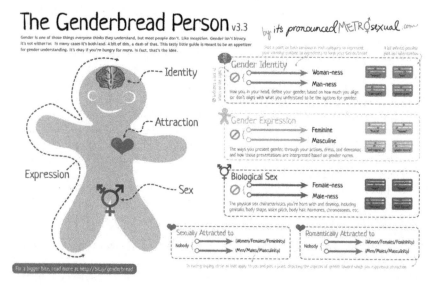

Figure 2.1 First published in *The Social Justice Advocate's Handbook: A Guide to Gender* by Sam Killermann (http://samuelkillermann.com/)

Opening Illustration

In 1972, at the heart of the second wave of feminist movement, Lois Gould published the fictional tale, "The Story of X: A Fabulous Child's Story," in *Ms. Magazine*. The story's narrator describes an imaginary parenting scenario in which a baby is born, named "x," and under the guidance of scientists is deliberately raised in a gender-neutral way. The

24

child is not subject to feminizing or masculinizing influences through toy selection and clothing coded as feminine or masculine, and is coparented equally by opposite-sex parents. The story calls attention to the many gendered messages we experience on a daily basis: "bouncing it up in the air and saying how strong and active it was, they'd be treating it more like a boy than an X. But if all they did was cuddle it and kiss it and tell it how sweet and dainty it was, they'd be treating it more like a girl than an X. On page 1654 of the Official Instruction Manual, the scientists prescribed: 'plenty of bouncing and plenty of cuddling, both, X ought to be strong and sweet and active. Forget about dainty altogether'" (Gould). Gould's ultimate moral was that parenting that drew from a range of human virtues would produce well-adjusted, functional children who were free to express themselves and pursue their interests regardless of whether those expressions and pursuits were coded as masculine or feminine.

A contemporary version of this fictional tale made news headlines recently, with news journalists documenting the stories of two contemporary couples[1] whose decision not to reveal their baby's sex (up until the child reached school age) earned them a great deal of public scorn and attention.[2] As one of the parents, Beck Laxton, said in an interview with the *Cambridge News*, "I wanted to avoid all that stereotyping. Stereotypes seem fundamentally stupid. Why would you want to slot people into boxes?" Laxton, a UK-based online editor, and her partner, Kieran Cooper, decided to keep Sasha's sex a secret when he was still in the womb. The birth announcement stated the gender-neutral name of their child but skipped the big reveal. Up until recently, the couple only told a few close friends and family members that Sasha was a boy and managed to keep the rest of the world "in the dark." Another couple announced the arrival of their baby with an email that read "We've decided not to share Storm's sex for now—a tribute to freedom and choice in place of limitation, a stand up to what the world could become in Storm's lifetime (a more progressive place? . . .)."

Gould's story and the contemporary version of the Fabulous X simultaneously illustrate how gender is encoded and maintained through a variety of strong social cues (i.e., naming practices, parenting responsibilities, toys, clothing, games, interpersonal interactions, and media exposure) and the way that people struggle to carve out space and identities that resist normative constructions of gender. This chapter explores how a social constructionist approach to gender is a key feature of a feminist theoretical lens.

A *feminist stance* understands gender as a system of privilege and oppression; it also assumes that gender is socially constructed, and is deeply interested in mapping out how, where, and to what effect.

Why a Threshold Concept?

A core premise of feminist scholarship is that gender and sex are distinct from each other, and that our gender identities are socially constructed and not immutable. Key to this concept is that ideas and constructions of gender change across time, between and within cultures, and even within one's lifespan. The specific ways that gender is socially constructed at any given time also serve the purpose of establishing and perpetuating *sexism*, defined as prejudice and discrimination based on sex. Furthermore, racial, ethnic, and cultural identities frame expectations for appropriate gendered behavior, as does social class and sexuality. Simply put, feminist scholars focus on how gender is socially constructed, and to what ends, and they are simultaneously interested in how social constructions of gender are shaped by issues of race, class, age, ability, and sexual identity. This threshold concept, then, is deeply intertwined both with the concept of privilege and oppression, which is the focus of Chapter 3, and the concept of intersectionality, which is the focus of Chapter 4.

Framing Definitions and Related Concepts

Social Constructionism

One of the early foundational theories underpinning a social constructionist approach is C. Wright Mills's articulation of the concept of the **sociological imagination**. In his 1959 book of the same name, Mills argues that "the individual can understand his own experience and gauge his own fate only by locating himself within his period, that he can know his own chances in life only by becoming aware of those of all individuals in his circumstances" (5). Mills's claims became the foundation of social science and sociology as a discipline. As Mills contended, "The sociological imagination enables us to grasp history and biography and the relations between the two within society" (6). As one of the foundations of feminist theory, **social constructionism** can be distinguished from other theories about sex and gender that are used to explain gender role socialization and how gendered systems are created and maintained. There are several hallmark concepts that distinguish a social constructionist approach to gender.

Sex and Gender

The "Genderbread Person" image that opens this chapter—and the accompanying controversies around it—is a case in point of the unsettled social understanding of the relationship between biological sex and the various ways that gender is created, expressed, and defined. What the image attempts to do is complicate our understanding of a binary gender system—boys and girls, men and women—and present a more varied spectrum of elements that make up sex, gender, and sexuality.

Although most scholars acknowledge that gender and sex exist on a continuum, a simple definition pulls apart these two commonly conflated terms into "sex," which focuses on the biological, genetic, and physiological features of males and females, and "gender," which characterizes the behavioral (and changeable/evolving) characteristics that we define as feminine and masculine. Physical features of sex include reproductive organs and secondary sex characteristics that develop at puberty, such as average difference and variation in muscle-to-fat ratios between men and women, and growth in body and facial hair. Gender, in contrast, is shaped by behavioral cues and social codes that are coded as "masculine" or "feminine." In the social constructionist understanding of gender, then, gender is performative, that is, something you "do" rather than something that is built into or programmed into you.

The work of feminist sociologist Judith Lorber serves as a touchstone in this area. Her work helpfully provides a number of terms that flesh out the idea of gender as a social construction. She makes clear that gendering is a *process* that has many dimensions and that occurs over time: first, there is the *assignment* of sex and gender, which quickly becomes a

gender status, according to Lorber, through naming, clothing, and the choice of children's toys and room decor. From there, children continue to be socialized into their gender, developing a **gender identity,** which is a person's gendered sense of self. The expression of that gendered sense of self is referred to as one's **gender comportment,** which Susan Stryker defines as "bodily actions such as how we use our voices, cross our legs, hold our heads, wear our clothes, dance around the room, throw a ball, walk in high heels" (12). This category is referred to as **gender expression** in the Genderbread figure that opens the chapter. Lorber also uses the term **gender display,** defined as the presentation of self as a kind of gendered person through dress, cosmetics, adornments, and both permanent and reversible body markers.

A social constructionist approach to gender rejects the belief that there are only two sexes and two genders, arguing instead that our current binary **sex/gender system** is itself a social construction. Powerful evidence for this argument comes from the **intersex** community (those who are themselves intersexed, parents of intersex children, and researchers who focus on intersexuality). The Intersex Society of North America defines intersex as "a general term used for a variety of conditions in which a person is born with a reproductive or sexual anatomy that doesn't seem to fit the typical definitions of female or male." While it has been difficult to get a handle on how frequently intersex babies are born, Anne Fausto-Sterling estimates that intersex births account for 1.7 percent of all births. She helpfully puts this into perspective: "a city of 300,000 would have 5,100 people with varying degrees of intersexual development. Compare this with albinism, another relatively uncommon human trait but one that most readers can probably recall having seen. Albino births occur much less frequently than intersexual births—in only about 1 in 20,000 babies" (51–53). For those who believe that sex and gender are binary—that there are only two possibilities, male and female—intersex babies are "really" male or female, and medical management, including genital surgery, can bring their physical appearance in line with their "true" sex. By contrast, Anne Fausto-Sterling and many others argue that the birth of intersex babies indicates that sex and gender are not binary, that is, that there are more than two categories, male and female, and she envisions a future (an admittedly utopic one) in which a wide range of gender identities and expressions would be permitted, even encouraged. Toward this end, Fausto-Sterling and the Intersex Society of North America call for an end to infant genital surgery on intersex babies, both because they feel strongly that decisions about making any permanent changes to the appearance and sexual function of intersex people should be made by themselves, or at least in consultation with them, *and* because the genital surgeries reinforce the idea that there are really only two sexes. Cheryl Chase, founder of the Intersex Society of North America and herself born intersex, argues that "children should be made to feel loved and accepted in their unusual bodies" (Weil).

Recent legal victories would seem to suggest some small steps toward Fausto-Sterling's vision: India, Pakistan and New Zealand now recognize a third gender, and in 2013, Germany enacted a law that allows parents to refrain from marking "M" or "F" on their intersex baby's birth certificate. The law was intended to allow parents to defer the decision and allow the child to decide later on whether to identify as male or female; however, the law also stipulates that a child could continue to identify as intersex. In a move that echoes the Gould story that opens this chapter, Germans can choose to use an "X" in the gender field of their passport.

While most people experience congruence between their **gender assignment**, gender identity, and gender expression, this is not automatically the case, and a growing number of people are exploring other identities and ways of being, and demanding legal recognition for their right to do so. The term **transgender** has many complex meanings and nuances, but a starting point is that it is used to describe an individual for whom there is a lack of congruence between their gender assignment and gender identity. In *Transgender History*, Susan Stryker uses the term "to refer to people who move away from the gender they were assigned at birth, people who cross over (*trans-*) the boundaries constructed by their culture to define and contain that gender" (1). While it used to be more common for that movement to remain within the boundaries of the binary gender system, that is, by seeking sex reassignment surgery and transitioning from identifying as a man to identifying as a woman (or vice versa), many trans* people today are increasingly identifying themselves and staking out territory outside the binary altogether. As Stryker points out, some people "seek to resist their birth-assigned gender without abandoning it," whereas others "seek to create some kind of new gender location" (19). Trans* people may or may not modify their bodies using surgery and/or hormones and may or may not seek legal recognition for their gender identity if it does not match the sex and gender they were assigned at birth.

Conversely, the terms **cisgender** and **cissexual** are used to describe people who experience congruence between their gender assignment and gender identity. Stryker points out that the creation of this term helps to name and mark that experience rather than assuming it as the norm. She writes, "The idea behind the terms is to resist the way that 'woman' or 'man' can mean 'nontransgendered woman' or 'nontransgendered man' by default, unless the person's transgender status is explicitly named" (22).

Social media have also responded to the expanding understanding of gender identity that has emanated from a variety of sources, including the intersex and the trans* communities. For example, Facebook in 2014 changed the gender field of its profile options to allow for a wider range of user selections, moving from the binary "male/female" options to roughly 50 options including "cisgender," "trans male," "androgynous," and "genderqueer," among others (Henn). Although the opportunity to choose one's online gender identity, along with the legal recognition of a third gender in several countries, indicates that change is afoot and many people are actively working to create more cultural space for life beyond the binary, this is not to downplay or diminish the realities of **transphobia**, which Julia Serano defines as "an irrational fear of, aversion to, or discrimination against people whose gendered identities, appearances, or behaviors deviate from societal norms." Even as many, especially younger people, are actively embracing gender fluidity, there are powerful forces that are working actively to police the boundaries of sex and gender. A recent incident in the state of Colorado highlights the uneven nature of change; the Girl Scouts (GSUSA) found themselves under attack over the inclusion of Bobby Montoya, a grade-school aged trans girl. In fact, Bobby's desire to join the Girl Scouts was initially thwarted by a troop leader who cited Bobby's "boy parts" as a barrier to joining, but that decision was quickly reversed based on national GSUSA policy. The FAQ section of the GSUSA website states that "if the child is recognized by the family and school/community as a girl and lives culturally as a girl, then Girl Scouts is an organization that can serve her in a setting that is both emotionally and physically safe." When Bobby's story hit the news, however, a group calling itself Honest Girl Scouts encouraged a cookie-buying boycott, citing GSUSA's "bias for transgenders [*sic*]."

Gender Socialization

Having made an initial pass through an explanation of the distinction between sex and gender, as well as what gender *is* or consists of, we can now ask and answer the question of where and how we learn about gender in our culture. Where do we learn what it means to be a boy or girl in our culture, in terms of appearance and behavior, and what are the cues and messages that we receive, both implicitly and explicitly? That is, we can begin to think about where, but also how, we are socialized into our gender. Some of the primary sites and arenas of **gender socialization** include the family, education, religion, popular culture and the media, sports, and the legal and criminal justice systems. What follows are a few examples of how these societal institutions serve as a site of gender socialization (note: institutions as sites and mechanisms for structuring systems of privilege and oppression will be discussed in Chapter 3 as well).

Education

K–12 education is organized around values of compliance and obedience, a fact that has gendered implications. As Sadker and Sadker explain, boys are more likely to be overdiagnosed with behavioral and emotional problems such as Attention Deficit Disorder, whereas girls' higher overall average grades and lower test scores may reflect what they note is an educational setting that values "following the rules, being quiet, and conforming to school norms" (78). In this way, particular behaviors are rewarded even if they are not ultimately those that will lead to "success" beyond school and in other settings that prize assertiveness and risk-taking behaviors. Ideas about appropriate areas of academic study for boys and girls are often reinforced in educational settings as well.

Family Structures and the Workplace

Social and policy structures that assume female caretaking and the primacy of men's careers send strong reinforcing messages and logistical cues about the responsibility for child care as a female one. For example, paid family and medical leave for the birth or adoption of a child (or to care for sick or elderly family members) does not exist on a standard national level in the United States (although it is common in other industrialized countries), and the status of the U.S. leave program as unpaid reinforces the notion that expectant women can rely on the income of a (usually) male partner to support them during childbirth and throughout infancy. When these are heavily gendered responsibilities, messages about who belongs in the public sphere and who belongs in the private sphere are clear. Children also learn what is considered "women's work" and what is considered "men's work" by observing both the amount and kind of domestic and unpaid work performed by their parents and caregivers. Although the amount of housework performed by women has gone down over the last 30 years, and the amount of housework performed by men has gone up, a significant gap remains between the average weekly hours spent by men and women engaged in these tasks, with women still spending roughly twice as much time as men. As the Bureau of Labor Statistics notes, women do 10.8 hours more unpaid household labor than men, and among 25- to 34-year-olds, women perform 31.7 hours of household work compared with men's 15.8 ("Hours"). And while recent studies show that men's share of meal preparation and child care has increased, the biggest gap is around cleaning.

These messages are not just conveyed through observation of adults, however; children are also socialized into their gender through the chores they are (or aren't) asked to perform around the house, and the

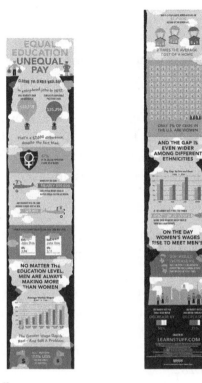

Figure 2.2 LearnStuff.com

money they may receive in the form of an allowance. The Allstate Foundation's 2014 Teens and Personal Finance Survey revealed that more boys than girls reported receiving an allowance from their parents (67% v. 59%). A 2007 study by the University of Michigan Institute for Social Research found that "girls spend more time doing housework than they do playing, while boys spend about 30 percent less time doing household chores than girls and more than twice as much time playing." And finally, several studies have shown that in families where both boys and girls get allowances, boys' allowances are higher. Taken together, these findings suggest that chores and allowances are key sites of boys' and girls' gender socialization.

Religions

Most major religions are based on a heavy foundation of **masculine god language,** and masculine iconography as omniscient and omnipotent; major religions are centered on male prophets and gods and around strict rules for male and female conduct, particularly regarding sexuality, reproduction, and marriage. Masculine god-language that refers to deities as "Him" and "Our Heavenly Father" reinforce an image of an all-powerful male ruler. Religious texts as well often communicate oppressive notions about gender relationships, such as Biblical passages including:

> "Women should keep silence in churches. For they are not permitted to speak, but should be subordinate, as even the law says" (1 Cor. 14:34).
>
> "I would have you know that the head of every man is Christ; and the head of the woman is the man; and the head of Christ is God" (1 Cor. 11:3).
>
> "Wives, submit yourselves unto your own husbands, as it is fit in the Lord" (Col. 3:18).
>
> "Let the woman learn in silence with all subjection. But I suffer not a woman to teach, nor to usurp authority over the man, but to be in silence" (1 Tim. 2:11–15).

Further, in a number of faiths, women are excluded from religious practices. For example, Hindu women perform rituals of self-denial, such as fasting, in order to create positive energy and power for their husbands. The self-sacrifice of a woman for her husband is understood to be a religious offering. Men do not perform such rituals for their wives (Burn). Women are often also excluded from leadership positions. Female ministers, bishops, priests, rabbis, mullahs, gurus, or sadhus remain relatively rare or nonexistent in many religious traditions. Children who attend worship services learn by observing the roles played by both children and adult men and women in those places of worship, and they also absorb explicit and implicit messages about their "proper" roles.

Mass Media, Popular Culture, and Material Culture

From birth, children are exposed to gendered messages in the form of pink or blue blankets and baby name signs, in the gendered division of toy store aisles, and in TV shows geared toward girls or boys, as well as the dominance of male characters in children's media. Regarding children's media, research from the Geena Davis Institute on Gender in Media found that girl characters are outnumbered by boy characters by a ratio of 3 to 1. Another example comes from looking at recipients of Best Picture Oscar awards. For example, films that have been praised and rewarded in the film industry are almost universally male centered. A brief review of the films receiving the Best Picture award over the last two decades demonstrates that male-centered narratives are most typically perceived as worthy of adulation.

For example, the majority of the films center on a heroic male protagonist who overcomes a significant obstacle (such as *The Departed*'s focus on the main character's navigation of his life as a double agent; *A Beautiful Mind*, documenting the main character as a genius suffering from a mental illness; or Oscar Schindler's acts of heroism during the Holocaust in *Schindler's List*). Films such as *The Silence of the Lambs*, while including a central female character, largely are driven by her interaction with or attempts to understand a more significant male character (in that film, Hannibal Lecter). Other filmic conventions rewarded include vengeance stories, such as a male character seeking out revenge for a wrong done to a woman (*Unforgiven*); or the emotional life of a male character presumed to be of depth and thus interest to a viewer, such as *The English Patient* or *American Beauty*. Films centered on war or battle are also overrepresented (such as *Braveheart*, *Platoon*, *Gladiator*, *Lord of the Rings*, *The Hurt Locker*, and *Schindler's List*) relative to their overall proportion of film plots. This emphasis on male-centered narratives and male-identified events and activities (war, battle, math, detective work, the Old West) communicate strong messages about what is culturally valuable and what (and who) is interesting. On a similar note, a recent analysis of the roles played by the winners of the Best Actress Oscar showed that almost a third of the winners played roles that were defined primarily through relationship to a man or men; that is, as wives,

Table 2.1 List of Best Picture Award Winners

2012 – *Argo*	1999 – *American Beauty*
2011 – *The Artist*	1998 – *Shakespeare in Love*
2010 – *The King's Speech*	1997 – *Titanic*
2009 – *The Hurt Locker*	1996 – *The English Patient*
2008 – *Slumdog Millionaire*	1995 – *Braveheart*
2007 – *No Country for Old Men*	1994 – *Forrest Gump*
2006 – *The Departed*	1993 – *Schindler's List*
2005 – *Crash*	1992 – *Unforgiven*
2004 – *Million Dollar Baby*	1991 – *The Silence of the Lambs*
2003 – *The Lord of the Rings: The Return of the King*	1990 – *Dances With Wolves*
2002 – *Chicago*	1989 – *Driving Miss Daisy*
2001 – *A Beautiful Mind*	1988 – *Rain Man*
2000 – *Gladiator*	1987 – *The Last Emperor*
	1986 – *Platoon*

mothers, sisters, daughters, or girlfriends. Tellingly, there was no parallel "relational" category for the Best Actor winners. The good news here is that this seems to be changing over time. Halle Berry's role in *Monster's Ball* in 2001 was the last to be added to this category of "relational" roles. In addition, in the last decade more films featuring central female characters have been among Best Picture nominees, including *Million Dollar Baby* (2004), *Little Miss Sunshine* (2006), *Juno* (2007), *Precious* (2009), *Black Swan* (2010), and *The Help* (2011). And in terms of box-office success, as of May 2014, two of the top three movie releases of 2013 featured female protagonists: *Hunger Games: Catching Fire* and *Frozen*, evidence which counters the notion that male viewers are not interested in paying to see films that feature female protagonists and female-centered storylines. Recall the Case Study in Chapter One on the Bechdel test as a way of critically examining gender and film.

Athletics

Sports is a primary site of gender socialization, especially for adolescents. Cheerleading in its earliest incarnations was a male activity, developed

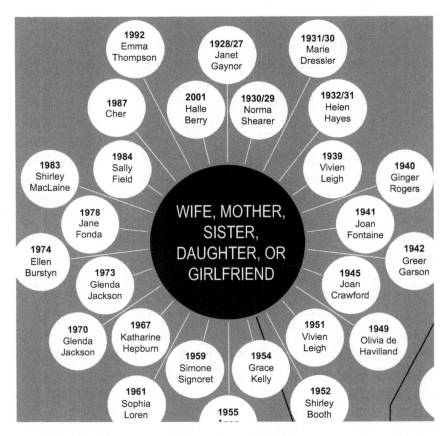

1992 Emma Thompson

1928/27 Janet Gaynor

1931/30 Marie Dressler

1987 Cher

2001 Halle Berry

1930/29 Norma Shearer

1932/31 Helen Hayes

1983 Shirley MacLaine

1984 Sally Field

1939 Vivien Leigh

1940 Ginger Rogers

WIFE, MOTHER, SISTER, DAUGHTER, OR GIRLFRIEND

1978 Jane Fonda

1941 Joan Fontaine

1974 Ellen Burstyn

1973 Glenda Jackson

1945 Joan Crawford

1942 Greer Garson

1970 Glenda Jackson

1967 Katharine Hepburn

1959 Simone Signoret

1954 Grace Kelly

1951 Vivien Leigh

1949 Olivia de Havilland

1961 Sophia Loren

1955

1952 Shirley Booth

Figure 2.3 Infographic by Jan Diehm for the *Huffington Post.*

in 1898 as "pep clubs" (International). Charged with generating crowd enthusiasm, cheer clubs were male-only until 1923, but by the 1940s women became the majority of cheerleaders in the United States. Today, 96% of cheerleaders are female (Bettis and Adams). Cheerleading is suggestive of male-centeredness; as a "corollary" or "add-on" to, initially, exclusively male athletic events, primarily football and basketball, cheer-leading has evolved to function as a method of (1) drawing attention to the athletic activities and achievements of a group of culture-dominant men, and (2) demanding particular highly compliant, traditionally fem-inine, and surface-focused standards from its female participants. By the 1970s, the emergence of professional cheerleading squads popularized the erotic image of the female cheerleader and her support of the athletic prowess of her team. As Bettis and Adams observe, "erotic tensions . . . creep into the language, practices, and policies of cheerleading squads at all levels, from preadolescent All-Star squads to collegiate competitive squads" (123). With current cheerleading choreography including what Bettis and Adams call "sexually suggestive" and "sexually provocative" moves, cheerleading becomes outward-looking in its emphasis on drawing attention to male athletics and in the efforts of female participants to garner social status through male attention to the often erotic performance of cheerleading routines. Competitive cheer has evolved as an offshoot of traditional cheerleading; its growing popularity can be seen in movies like *Bring it On* (2000) and the television show *Glee*, which features an award-winning squad called the Cheerios. Many people consider competitive cheer to be a sport, and organizing bodies within the field have petitioned the NCAA to officially recognize it as such on the collegiate level. Some cynically see the push to have competitive cheer recognized as a collegiate sport as a way for universities to comply technically with Title IX regulations while not supporting more traditional sports for women athletes. Proponents of recognizing cheerleading as a sport argue that competitive cheer is highly athletic, and that those participating in it run the risk of incurring severe sports-related injuries. But while competitive cheer draws its own audience (as opposed to being on the sidelines of another sporting event), it arguably maintains the requirement of traditionally feminine appearance and sexually suggestive choreography.

Electoral Politics

In the United States, women are extremely underrepresented in elected office relative to their numbers in the general population. As of 2014, according to the Center for American Women and Politics, women represent 18.5% of Congress and 24.2% of state legislators; only 10% of governors are women. These mirror global numbers: as recent data show, 15% of the world's lawmakers are female in 2003; in 2012, that number was 18.6%. The United States ranks 59th among 125 countries with female representatives. The United States, France, and Japan all lag behind 13 sub-Saharan countries. Many countries have no female representatives or less than 5% (e.g., Yemen, Vanuatu, Tonga, Saudi Arabia, Samoa, Qatar, Iran, Marshall Islands, and Egypt). The patterns and expectations are set at an early age, with many high schools and universities electing fewer young women to student government positions. For example, in 2013 at Phillips Academy, an elite prep school in Andover, Massachusetts, students spoke out about the lack of female student leadership since the school opened its ranks to female students in 1973. According to a *New York Times* article written about the campus controversy, only four young women have been elected to the position of school president in the past 40 years. In an effort to increase female representation in student government, the school's administration adopted a copresident model in the hope that mixed-gender groups would run for office. Although the intended effect was not produced in 2013 (when two young men were elected), each pair of finalists in the 2014 election consisted of one young man and one young woman, ensuring the election of a woman to the copresidency. At the postsecondary level, the American Student Government Association estimates that 40% of student presidents are women, also noting, however, that that number does not distinguish between two-year and four-year campuses; the assumption is that the number of women presidents on four-year campuses is lower (Johnson). A May 2013 report by the Center for Information and Research on Civic Learning and Engagement adds nuance to the discussion of women's underrepresentation in political office by pointing out that although women are "severely underrepresented at virtually all levels of elected office," girls and young women outpace their male peers "on many indicators of civic engagement, including volunteering, membership in community associations, and voting" (Kawashima-Ginsburg and Thomas 2). The report attempts to explain what leads to and creates the gender gap in leadership, and several of those factors clearly stem from the differing gender socialization of boys and girls. More specifically, they point to a gap in both confidence and expectations. They cite survey data from the Higher Education Research Institute that shows that women in their first year of college "are far less likely to claim personal characteristics such as leadership and public speaking skills, competitiveness, social skills, and popularity, all of which are commonly named characteristics of a political leader," (4) and they note that the gap has not narrowed in the past almost 50 years. Finally, they cite a study from American University that found that 30% of young college women had been encouraged to run for office, compared to 40% of young college men. More specifically, women "were less likely to be encouraged by parents, grandparents, teachers, religious leaders, coaches, and even friends" (6). In sum, both the implicit and explicit gendered messages boys and girls receive about political leadership shape the paths they pursue in adolescence and adulthood.

Rape Culture and the Legal System

Men's violence against women continues to be a threat to the health and safety of women worldwide, providing strong social cues about women's and men's roles, masculinity and femininity, and serving as an important part of maintaining patriarchal culture. Both bell hooks and Jackson Katz have argued that violent masculinity is at the foundation of patriarchal culture, based on, as hooks states, "the belief that it is acceptable for a more powerful individual to control others through various forms of coercive force." Violence, *or the threat of violence*, is a powerful tool in maintaining gender inequality. As a part of gender socialization, it's important to note that **rape culture** (see inset box) (and the accompanying response or lack of response from legal and law enforcement structures) provide strong cues about men's and women's roles. Data from the United Nations and from the Center for Disease Control show that 40% to 70% of women murdered in the United States, Canada, Australia, and Israel were killed by their husbands or male partners. Further, 73% of sexual assaults were perpetrated by a nonstranger—38% of perpetrators were a friend or acquaintance of the victim, 28% were intimate with the victim, and 7% were another relative (National Crime Victimization Survey, 2005). In the United States, approximately 22% of black women, 18.8% of white non-Hispanic women, and 14.6% Hispanic women have experienced rape at some point in their lives. More than one-quarter of women (26.9%) who identified as American Indian or as Alaska Native and 1 in 3 women (33.5%) who identified as multiracial non-Hispanic reported rape victimization in their lifetime. A

2014 research study reported on the "normalization of sexual violence among young girls and women" and concluded that many young women view sexual violence and accompanying behaviors such as objectification, abuse, and harassment by boys and men as a normal part of daily life (McDonough). The original sociological study by Heather Hlavka focused on explaining why few girls and women report sexual violence, offering "normalization" as one explanation, as well as the lack of confidence young women have in authority and the lack of support from other girls and women. The "naturalization" of violent masculinity also played a role. As a form of social control, then, the constant threat of violence (sexual, physical, or otherwise) is one way that male dominance is enforced and reinforced in overlapping areas of women's lives and where gendered qualities such as female compliance, cooperation, and passivity are scripted.

Rape Culture

Lynn Phillips, a lecturer in Communication at UMass Amherst, offers a definition of rape culture, calling it ". . . a culture in which dominant cultural ideologies, media images, social practices, and societal institutions support and condone sexual abuse by normalizing, trivializing and eroticizing male violence against women and blaming victims for their own abuse" (Kacmarek and Geffre). The film *The Bro Code: How Contemporary Culture Creates Sexist Men* highlights the ubiquity of humorous treatments of rape and sexual assault in popular culture and mass media; one only has to peruse a newspaper, news magazine, or Internet news site to identify many daily examples of rape and sexual assault, including gang rape. As *The Bro Code* notes, 99% of rapists are men, and popular shows such as *Family Guy* and comedians such as Daniel Tosh of the show *Tosh* routinely take comic approaches to rape that, instead of deconstructing or critiquing rape culture, endorse or embrace it. The "Rape Joke Supercut"[3] short at the Women's

Media Center highlights the difference between these two types of rape jokes: See also Jessica Valenti's "Anatomy of a Successful Rape Joke';[4] Kate Harding's "15 Rape Jokes that Work";[5] and Lindy West's "How To Make a Rape Joke"[6] for trenchant critiques of this element of rape culture.

A social constructionist approach argues that our gender identity, that is, our personal understanding of our own gender, is shaped by the intersection of experience and institutions and organizations. We receive implicit and explicit messages through our interactions with each of these institutions that fundamentally shape our understandings of ourselves and our beliefs about the world.

Gender Ranking

In *The Gender Knot: Unraveling Our Patriarchal Legacy*, Johnson argues that *androcentrism*, or centering on and valuing of those qualities associated with masculinity, is a part of our cultural norms. This male-centeredness becomes visible through a close look at how status and power are distributed in our society. With positions of power that are male-dominated, and higher value attached to masculine personality traits like "control, strength, competitiveness, toughness, coolness under pressure, logic, forcefulness, decisiveness, rationality, autonomy, self-sufficiency, and control over any emotion that interferes with other core values (such as invulnerability) . . . these male identified qualities are associated with the work valued most in patriarchal societies—business, politics, war, athletics, law, and medicine" (7). This **gender ranking** is often framed as both biological in origin and immutable, with masculine qualities defined in opposition to—and more culturally valued than—feminine qualities.

A social constructionist approach to gender also argues that masculinity and femininity are defined in relation to one another. More specifically, masculinity is defined in opposition to femininity. As

Table 2.2 Stereotypical Gender Qualities

"Masculine" Qualities	*"Feminine" Qualities*
aggressive/assertive	passive
logical/analytical	indirectly aggressive ("catty")
physically strong, athletic	sensitive
responsible	other-oriented
protective	physically weak/er
self-oriented	compromising
emotionally unexpressive	emotionally expressive
in control	collaborative
authoritative	submissive
invulnerable	nurturing
sexually aggressive	chaste or pure

Raewyn Connell puts it, "'Masculinity' does not exist except in contrast with 'femininity'" (252). In *Full Frontal Feminism*, Jessica Valenti puts a finer point on it: "masculinity is defined as whatever *isn't* womanly" (185). The oppositional and relational nature of socially constructed masculinity and femininity are evident in Table 2.2.

Within a sex/gender system that privileges masculinity, a certain latitude is given to girls and women to emulate masculinity. In other words, we have space in our culture for girls to be "tomboys," because there is a certain logic in many people's minds to why a girl would want to adopt masculine styles of dress, behavior, and play. But because femininity is devalued, boys who are termed "sissies" frequently endure merciless teasing. In adulthood, masculine styles of dress, within certain parameters, are open to women; think, for example, of the popularity of "boyfriend" jeans, chinos, sweaters, and button-down shirts. The same cannot be said of men's clothing; there is no parallel "girlfriend" styling of men's clothing. This point will be explored visually in the "Bodies" portion of the Anchoring Topics section.

But aside from clothing, the emulation of masculinity by adult women can be fraught. There is a double standard of behavior for men and women in the workplace and in politics, for example, where the same behavior is judged very differently depending on whether the person engaging in the behavior is a man or woman. Sheryl Sandberg's Lean In organization is attempting to raise awareness of one manifestation of this double standard with its "Ban Bossy" campaign. As the campaign's website puts it, "When a little boy asserts himself, he's called a 'leader.' When a little girl does the same, she risks being branded 'bossy.'" Closely related to this concept of a **gendered double standard** of behavior is the idea of the **double bind**, whereby women in the public sphere are faced with two less-than-desirable options of adhering to or rejecting feminine gender norms, risking negative repercussions either way. Amanda Fortini captured this double bind in an article she wrote about the 2008 U.S. presidential race, in which Hillary Clinton sought the Democratic presidential nomination and Sarah Palin was the Republican vice presidential candidate. Clinton's style was deemed more masculine, whereas Palin's was more traditionally feminine, but both received negative media attention. Fortini's title: "The 'Bitch' and the 'Ditz' (How the Year of the Woman Reinforced the Two Most Pernicious Sexist Stereotypes and Actually Set Women Back"). This gendered double standard also has everything to do with race and class; traditional femininity is often implicitly coded as both white and middle class. African American women in positions of power in the workplace and in politics, for example, have to negotiate a gendered double standard that is also interwoven with racial stereotypes, such as the Angry Black Woman trope.

Reimagining Masculinity

Gender ranking serves the purpose of maintaining and perpetuating *sexism*, that is to say, a system of male dominance. However, there is a growing realization that boys and men often experience deep and lasting harm as a result of adhering to, striving to adhere to, or failing to adhere to, the very masculine gender norms that form the foundation of sexism. Paul Kivel's articulation of both the contents of the **act-like-a-man box,** as well as its purpose and function, has been key in this area. He calls it a box to emphasize the rigidity, narrowness and confining aspects of the social construction of masculinity. He writes, "it feels like a box, a 24-hour-a-day, seven-day-a-week box that society tells boys they must fit themselves into. One reason we know it's a box is because every time a boy tries to step out he's pushed back in with names like wimp, sissy, mama's boy, girl, fag, nerd, punk, mark, bitch, and others even more graphic. Behind those names is the threat of violence" (148). Gender norms of both masculinity and femininity are maintained through many mechanisms, including through the "policing" of people's behavior. Kivel points out that this policing of boys can come from other boys, but also from girls, who "don't seem to like us when we step out of the box" (148). This policing can also come from adults, who "seem convinced that if they 'coddle' us, we will be weak and vulnerable" (148). A graphic illustration of the policing of the "act-like-a-man-box" can be found in the story of a young boy in Raleigh, North Carolina, who attempted suicide in February 2014 after a long period of being bullied because he is a fan of the television show "My Little Pony." Feminine gender norms in girls are also policed by both genders and by both peers and adults. When girls and women police other girls and women, this is referred to as **horizontal hostility**, a phenomenon that will be discussed more fully in Chapter 3.

A growing body of psychological and medical research has linked boys' and men's adherence to traditional masculine gender norms with a number of connected negative outcomes: loss of intimate friendship, high rates of depression, and lower life expectancy. Regarding friendship, according to sociologist Lisa Wade, the qualities needed to extend and receive friendship are coded feminine in our culture, thus causing a gender role conflict for men. She writes, "To be close friends, men need to be willing to confess their insecurities, be kind to others, have empathy and sometimes sacrifice their own self-interest. 'Real men,' though, are not supposed to do these things. They are supposed to be self-interested, competitive, non-emotional, strong (with no insecurities at all), and able to deal with their emotional problems without help. Being a good friend, then, as well as needing a good friend, is the equivalent of being girly." She cites research by psychologist Niobe Way that found that younger boys report having close, intimate friendships with other boys, but that there is a shift around the age of 15 or 16, when boys "start reporting that they don't have friends and don't need them." Later in adulthood, however, many adult men report wanting intimate friendships but are not sure how to forge them. This example not only illustrates the limitations of adhering to traditional norms of masculinity, but it also reveals the need to consider how the social construction of masculinity changes across an individual's life span. Put differently, these example shows the importance of thinking about gender in relation to age.

Beyond identifying the limitations and harm of traditional masculinity, a growing number of men are making strides in their personal, professional, and activist lives toward reimagining masculinity. Guante, a hip hop artist, poet, and social justice educator has a spoken word piece, "Ten Responses to the Phrase 'Man Up,'" that resonates deeply with audiences. Another poet, Carlos Andres Gomez, published a book entitled *Man Up: Reimagining Modern Manhood* in 2012. Both men offer analysis of masculinity as a forced performance, make public declarations that they reject traditional masculinity, and instead claim for themselves a reimagined manhood that, as Guante puts it, entails having meaningful, emotional relationships with other men, admitting weakness, and being "strong in a way that isn't about physical power or dominance." Indeed, a huge emphasis of the work of men like Guante and Gomez, and groups like A Call to Men is reimagining masculinity toward the end of preventing violence, whether that's men's violence against women, against themselves, or against other men. Men's work to reimagine masculinity benefits girls and women, then, in the sense that it is focused on reducing violence against women, but it also benefits boys and men per se, in the sense that it can result in raising their quality of life, even as it may entail giving up some of the unearned privileges of masculinity.

The examples described in this section give a sense of how complex the gender landscape is in the 21st century. Many people, young and old, chafe against the restrictions of the gender binary that dictate that masculinity and femininity are relational and oppositional, and that masculinity is more highly valued. Simultaneously, however, other individuals, along with structural forces, work hard, in ways both visible and invisible, to shore up traditional norms and gendered expectations.

Learning Roadblock

"It's how you were raised." It can be tempting to analyze gender through a lens that imagines family structures are the sole and most important influence on a person's gender identity. Typically, these binary characterizations of gender are psychoanalytic in origin. Such theories originated from two different sources: **Freudian** views and those of other psychologists about how humans develop their sense of gender identity from deep roots in their childhood experience of family origin (experiences that are gendered); and theories that build on those psychological evolutions by positing essentialized views of masculine and feminine ways of developing psychologically, morally, and emotionally. Freudian theories undergird the psychological approach because of Freud's role in laying the groundwork for the study of the human psyche. Freud's theory of the Oedipus complex is sometimes used to explain the difference between male and female development of identity; in sum, Freud theorized that male children must individuate from their primary (female) caretaker and identify with the male parent in order to fully develop into an adolescent and adult. Freud's theory supposed a deep and unconscious basis in an unrealized sexual desire for the mother, one that is displaced by identification with the father. In contrast, female children do not need to individuate and become independent in their identity formation because their primary caretaker is the same-sex parent. Thus, boys and men, in this view, develop an identity characterized by separation, independence, and individuality whereas girls maintain an emphasis on identification, interdependence, and cooperation/mutuality.

However, as this chapter illustrates, families themselves are subject to and part of structural and cultural contexts that grant privileges to certain types of family structures and withhold it from others; parents themselves absorb and reproduce cultural values about gender. Family structures are part of larger institutional contexts that reproduce values around class, race, gender, sexuality, and other categories of identity—values that do not begin and end around the boundaries of families of origin. In short, it's not inaccurate to say that "how you were raised" shapes one's ideas about gender, but what *is* inaccurate is the assertion that the only necessary changes that need to be made to the structure of gender can be brought about through child-rearing practices.

Learning Roadblock

"Women and men are naturally _____*."* Historically and in our contemporary "commonplace" understandings of gender, *biology* holds a great deal of explanatory power, because physical differences between men and women are typically the first "cues" we experience about gender identity. Biological determinist explanations for gender role development are rooted in assumptions about men's greater average muscle mass and physical strength, in theories about genetics and hormonal differences between men and women, and in claims about reproductive strategies and the influence of women's reproductive life cycles, for example, on the development of their emotional and psychological priorities. Although the idea that gender and sex are biologically and genetically determined can have great explanatory power, scientific research as well as careful reflection reveal that many of the gendered behaviors we take for granted are actually highly socially constructed by the overlapping institutions we experience on a daily basis: the family, media, medical communities, religion, educational institutions, and so forth. The scientific and historical evidence of the malleability of gender—the wide range of sexualities across cultures; the range of expectations for masculine and feminine behavior across culture, time, and even an individual's life span; and the significant cultural energy spent on ensuring that boys and girls conform to particular gendered ideologies (through such mechanisms as gay and lesbian baiting, stigmatizing gender nonconforming behavior, and maintaining policies and practices that reward traditional gendered behaviors)—suggests that gender is not quite as "natural" as we suppose. A story featured in the online arts and culture magazine *Slate* showcases the strong explanatory power of biological and genetic explanations for gender differences. Calling attention to the media coverage of two studies published in the prestigious scholarly journal *Nature*, the story observes that "The *Huffington Post* quoted one of the studies' authors as saying that these 'special' genes 'may play a large role in differences between males and females.' Yet what the *Nature* articles *actually* show

is the exact opposite. The 12 genes residing on the Y chromosome exist to ensure sexual *similarity*" (Richardson). Although the original study findings emphasized sexual similarity, the story was "translated" to emphasize sexual difference—even though this was not actually borne out by the research.

Taken together, these interrelated framing concepts—social constructionism, the relationship between sex and gender, gender socialization, gender identity, gender expression, and gender ranking—are all part of understanding how a social constructionist approach is critical to feminist analysis.

Anchoring Topics through the Lens of Social Constructionism
Work and Family
One way of understanding the varying theories about gender construction is to look at the phenomenon of what is called **occupational segregation of labor**.

Overview of Gender Wage Gap/Occupational Segregation of Labor
As research from the Bureau of Labor Statistics and other sources consistently shows, occupations are strongly separated by gender; that is, particular segments of the labor market are occupied by women, and men are clustered in other labor segments. As the chart below illustrates in broad terms, particular types of work such as administrative and clerical work are fields that women are concentrated in; by contrast, production and craft work is largely done by male workers (91%).

A more fine-grained analysis suggests that very particular jobs such as secretaries and administrative assistants are mostly done by women (97%); work that involves small children is almost entirely performed by female workers (preschool teachers, 97.7%). By contrast, male-dominated occupations—those that typically pay significantly higher wages—are also as disproportionately dominated by men as those clerical positions are by women. Law enforcement officers are 84.5% male, 98% of automotive technical work is performed by men, and 97% of construction workers are men. Although occupational segregation of labor is a useful and robust topic through which to develop a more complicated picture of how, for example,

Occupation	Percentage of occupation that are men	Percentage of occupation that are women	Men		Women	
			Number (in thousands)	Percentage of all men employed in each occupation	Number (in thousands)	Percentage of all women employed in each occupation
Total...........................	...	...	67,334	100.0	59,787	100.0
Managerial.....................	54	46	11,005	16.3	9,387	15.7
Professional and technical......	46	54	12,063	17.9	13,552	23.3
Sales........................	52	48	7,601	11.3	6,953	11.6
Clerical and administrative support.................	21	79	3,751	5.6	14,128	23.6
Service.......................	39	61	6,465	9.6	10,066	16.8
Production and craft............	91	9	3,516	20.1	1,283	2.1
Operatives....................	76	24	9,302	13.8	3,007	5.0
Laborers......................	78	22	3,631	5.4	1,011	1.7

NOTE: The Index of Dissimilarity across all occupations in 2001 was 31.1.

Figure 2.4 Employed Persons 20 Years and Older in the Civilian Labor Force, By Occupation and Gender, 2001

Table 1 in Gabriel and Schmitz, "Gender Differences in Occupational Distributions Among Workers." See www.bls.gov/opub/mlr/2007/06/art2full.pdf for more information.

the **gender wage gap** is promoted and reproduced, for the purposes of this chapter the topic is discussed to illustrate various theories about how and why men and women occupy different labor market segments. As Gabriel and Schmitz explain, "31% of men or women (or a combination of percentages that add up to 31 percent) would have to change occupations for there to be complete gender equality in occupational distributions" (19). A social constructionist approach suggests that neither biological nor psychological assumptions accurately explain this segregation of occupations by gender, but rather the social construction of gender is both reflected and reinforced by the gendered segregation of labor.

Two terms that capture the issues in labor segregation include **vertical segregation of labor** and **horizontal segregation of labor**. For example, women are more likely to work in administrative and clerical positions whereas men are more likely to work in manufacturing and skilled labor; the wage gap is partly explained by women's clustering in lower-paying occupations; this is horizontal segregation of labor. Vertical segregation takes place simultaneously. For example, as the U.S. Department of Labor notes, more women than men work in professional fields, but women are more likely to be found in health and education professional fields and are paid less than those occupied by men, such as computer science and engineering. For example, "in 2010, only 8 percent of female professionals were employed in the relatively high-paying computer and engineering fields, compared with 43 percent of male professionals" (2). Other notable statistical information includes the higher proportion of female workers in part-time positions—as the Department of Labor data show, "Women who worked part-time made up 26 percent of all female wage and salary workers in 2010. In contrast, 13 percent of men in wage and salary jobs worked part-time" (2). Even within the same field, for example, medical professions, women are more likely to occupy lower-paying specialties such as public health or pediatrics, with men in higher-paid specialties like neurosurgery or internal medicine.

For women in elite and/or corporate positions, the construction of leadership itself may be gendered. For example, as Joan Williams and Rachel Dempsey discuss in *What Works for Women at Work: Four Patterns Working Women Need to Know*, even as women make up the majority of college students and have made inroads into many professions, positions of power remain starkly gendered male. Just 3.6% of Fortune 500 CEOs are women, for example (4), and just 15% of law firm partners are women. Workplace values centered on the unencumbered worker—historically, a male employee with few if any commitments outside the workplace—exert unequal pressures on male and female workers. Williams and Dempsey report that motherhood is the strongest trigger for bias: women with children are 79% less likely to be hired, only half as likely to be promoted, and earn a lot less money than women with identical resumes but without children, while this bias was untrue for men with children (5). A 2013 research study showed that women CEOs were more likely to be fired than their male counterparts—38% versus 27%, partly because they tend to be "riskier" hires brought in at times of corporate crisis (Duberman). Leadership qualities that require unencumbered workers and that are synonymous with traditionally male characteristics—self-assuredness, assertiveness, daring, and authoritative and commanding demeanors—all work against women and construct leadership work as masculine in nature.

But what kinds of explanations can be offered to make sense of this division of labor? As we outlined earlier as part of the learning roadblocks to understanding gender roles and gender socialization, biological, psychoanalytic, and social constructionist explanations have all been offered to make sense of the ways that people experience gender and gendering. How would each of these theories be used to explain the gendered segregation of labor?

- *biological determinist explanations*: A biological determinist would look at the occupational segregation of labor and locate the explanation for this division in genetic, biological, and evolutionary differences. The determinist might assert that because women are biologically responsible for reproduction, gestation, and lactation, as well as, because of these physiological realities, caring for children, that women are attracted to fields that make use of these "natural" dispositions. Lower-compensated and lower-status work such as early childhood education, child care, social work, secretarial work, and nursing are naturally suited to women's biological and evolutionary impulse toward caring for others. On the flip side, the physically demanding occupations such as logging and construction, for example, are occupied by men whose larger bodies and greater muscle strength make them physically suited for this work. Further, historical associations between men and logic as well as spatial skills (borne out by some neurological research) are used to justify the concentration of male workers in fields like law, architecture, and engineering.

- *psychoanalytic explanations*: The notion of a single psychoanalytic interpretation may be misleading—a range of perspectives, including Freudian, Jungian, and feminist interpretation such as work by Carol Gilligan have all influenced the development of psychological theories about gender. Psychoanalytic theories typically explain gender differentiation through relationships to others. For example, the (now dated) Freudian explanation centers on the gender identification that children experience with same-sex and opposite-sex parents, while other theories such as that of feminist Carol Gilligan (in response to Lawrence Kohlberg), challenge assumptions about moral development that emphasize independent decision-making based on a moral truth and disconnected from the needs of others as the pinnacle. By this logic, women (in general) were perpetually "immature" in their moral development because they were more likely to be driven by moral decision-making that accounted for the needs and feelings of others—the emotional or affective dimension—than by disconnected or objective applications of a moral principle. Psychoanalytic theories typically use essentialist assumptions about the moral or psychological orientation of men and women; as such, psychoanalytic explanations of occupational segregation focus on women's attraction to and suitability for relational care work and work guided by a sense of moral obligation to others. Conversely, more independence, or what Gilligan calls an "ethic of justice," is ascribed to men, which purportedly explains their attraction to fields that provide work that is objective, mechanical, or conducted independently.

- *social constructionist explanations/interpretations*: The prevailing approach to examining gender in most social science, interdisciplinary studies, humanities, and gender and women's studies courses is one of a social constructionist approach; that is, scholars assume that gender is neither natural nor immutable and point to the many institutions that shape our experiences. A social constructionist examination of the occupational segregation of labor would look at the ways that gender norms are expressed, communicated, and reinforced in ubiquitous ways throughout our lives. Children's exposure to workplaces in which 90% of their elementary school teachers are women and positions of authority even within the same setting (administrators and principals) are primarily male communicate powerful social messages about gender-appropriate career aspirations. Children experiencing animated media presenting stories about boys versus stories about girls at a ratio of 2 to 1 are also learning a powerful "unstated" assumption about gendered values.

Methods of untangling socially constructed gender norms from biological ones are complicated but still present a strong picture of the gap between "natural" or "biological" explanations and the realities of gender construction. For example, although there is a stereotype that boys and men are better at mathematics and related fields than girls are, the gap in performance on standardized tests between boys and girls has narrowed. Further, gaps in standardized math test scores vary by country—there are no sex differences between boys and girls in Russia, India, and Japan, and in Iceland and Japan, girls *outscored* boys on math tests. Were mathematical or other abilities fixed, we would not see cross-cultural variation at this rate, nor could we explain the increase in the number of women engineers from 0.3% of bachelor of science degrees in 1970 to 18.9% in 2012.

Further, cross-cultural expectations for gender vary widely, suggesting that, were genetics or biology at work in shaping an immutable set of expectations around men and women, boys and girls, we would not see so much variation between cultures and nations about what is considered masculine and what is considered feminine, as well as occupational segregation at the rate we see it in the United States.

Language, Images, and Symbols

As mentioned previously, a key aspect of assigning a gender to infants when they're born happens through the naming process (side note: many parents find out the sex of their baby, using ultrasound technology, in utero, which means that the process of gender assignment begins even *before* birth, particularly if parents-to-be take seriously the suggestion to talk to the fetus and begin addressing it by name while still in the womb). In the United States, the majority of given names are unambiguously gendered and considered appropriate only for girls or only for boys, although there are exceptions that add nuance to this discussion.

Studies have looked at how names that were historically considered masculine, like Ashley or Courtney, have been claimed and appropriated as girls' names. There are two related aspects of this sort of shift that connect to how gender operates in our culture. In terms of explaining *why* parents have chosen "boy" names for their daughters, it would seem that *gender ranking* comes into play here, meaning that within the logic of patriarchy, giving a girl a boy's name is an act of emulating privilege. That same "logic" also explains why there has been no parallel trend of parents choosing "girl" names for their sons; giving a boy a girl's name would be adopting the status of the less-valued gender (an interesting take on this issue can be found in Johnny Cash's classic country song, "A Boy Named Sue"). In terms of the *consequences* of parents choosing "boy" names for their daughters, we see that as more parents choose these names for their daughters, *fewer* parents choose those same names for their sons. In effect, then, there seems to be a tipping point; if too many parents choose a "masculine" name for their daughter, parents of male children avoid that name as it comes to be seen as feminine.

The popular website Nameberry, which tracks baby naming trends, has noted, however, that some new trends may be emerging. The site reports, in a 2012 post, seeing "parents 'reclaiming' for their sons unisex names that had veered girlward and names rising in tandem for both sexes." Another phenomenon that has yet to be quantified but has been reported anecdotally is that more parents are deliberately choosing gender-neutral names. Some parents, for example, are choosing not to find out the sex of their baby before its birth and decide on a name that could be used for either a boy or a girl.

Fast forwarding to adulthood, two recent studies that focus on gender bias in the workplace highlight the role that gendered names play in maintaining inequality. In one study referenced perhaps most notably by Sheryl Sandberg in her *Lean In*-based TED Talk, a business school professor gave his students a case study of a successful entrepreneur named Heidi Roizen, only he changed the name to Howard in one section. The professor, Francis Flynn, recalls "Before class, I had the students go online and rate their impressions of 'Roizen' on several dimensions. As you might expect, the results show that students were much harsher on Heidi than on Howard across the board. Although they think she's just as competent and effective as Howard, they don't like her, they wouldn't hire her, and they wouldn't want to work with her. As gender researchers would predict, this seems to be driven by how much they disliked Heidi's aggressive personality. The more assertive they thought Heidi was, the more harshly they judged her (but the same was not true for those who rated Howard)." The ultimate point here, of course, is not about names per se, but about the gendered double standard for workplace behavior. And yet the study is a stark reminder that names almost always convey our gender, and that gendered stereotyping and double standards often kick in on that basis alone.

In another recent study published in the *Proceedings of the National Academy of Sciences of the United States*, researchers asked natural sciences professors to rate the application materials of college students applying for a position as a laboratory manager. As with the Flynn study, the materials were identical in every way except for the name of the applicant: Jennifer or John. According to the study's authors, "Faculty participants rated the male applicant as significantly more competent and hirable than the (identical) female applicant. These participants also selected a higher starting salary and offered more career mentoring to the male applicant." A final study shows how names are not only gendered but racialized. In this study, published by the Social Science Research Network, researchers sent an identical e-mail to 6,500 professors across the United States. The researchers posed as prospective students asking to meet with the professor, with the only thing distinguishing the e-mails from one another being the names of those prospective students: Brad Anderson, Meredith Roberts, Lamar Washington, LaToya Brown, Juanita Martinez, Deepak Patel, Sonali Desai, Chang Wong, and Mei Chen. The findings: "faculty ignored requests from women and minorities at a higher rate than requests from Caucasian males, particularly in higher-paying disciplines and private institutions" (Milkman, Akinola, and Chugh). In other words, professors were more likely to respond to the prospective students who, based on their name, were perceived to be white and male. These examples clearly reveal some of the workplace and education-related implications of gendered and racialized naming practices, and how social constructionism is at work in large and small ways in communicating gender and race, as well as social roles and status.

A different way that gender comes into play in relation to naming has to do with the use of first names, last names, and/or titles in social interactions. Henley and Freeman argue that status is often communicated and reproduced by the levels of intimacy allowed to be expressed between two people depending on their social or employment status. Subordinates and superordinates have varying levels of freedom to address each other by first or last names, with the superordinate granted greater levels of familiarity than the subordinate. On a related note, many women professors note the tendency of students to refer to them either by first name or as "Mrs.," but not by their title of Doctor or Professor. While campus culture varies greatly across the United States, anecdotal evidence suggests a gendered dimension to this, with female professors consistently experiencing this phenomenon to a greater degree than their male colleagues.

Perhaps one of the most notable gendered controversies around naming, and socially communicated messages about naming and status, is the issue of (typically) heterosexual women changing their last name upon marriage. As Scheuble, Johnson, and Johnson explain, "The practice of married women taking their husband's last name originates from the patriarchal family system under which women were considered their husband's property" (282); yet, despite the many strides toward gender equity, this practice continues for the majority of women. Research and demographic information suggests that 80% to 90% or more of heterosexual women choose to take their husband's last name upon marriage, with women with greater levels of educational attainment and who marry at older ages less likely to adopt their husband's surname (Lockwood, Burton, and Boersma 827). As part of the social construction of gender roles, name changing remains a controversial practice among feminists, but a widely held cultural norm. One research study reported that women who change their surnames identified tradition and relationship bonding as key reasons for their decision, yet Lockwood, Burton, and Boersma concluded that concern for family dynamics—including upsetting extended family members with nontraditional naming choices—remained an important consideration for many women (837). That is, despite feminist critique of this patriarchal tradition, many women continue to adhere to traditional values. Some arguments suggest that with other strides in gender equity, taking a spouse's last name is not as meaningful now as in the past, such as Lynn Harris's argument in a 2003 *Salon* article, "Mrs. Feminist": "Today, a woman's decision to take her husband's name is not necessarily, or merely, 'retro.' When it comes to such political-slash-personal acts, the stakes have changed, and therefore so have the statements we're making with them. I would argue that we're not losing battles; we're choosing them. We're not retreating; we're showing, subtly, how far we've come." Although a clear minority, some women keep their name upon marriage or take their husband's name without ditching their own, through hyphenation. An even smaller number of couples have gone further, by having the husband take his wife's name (either alone or through hyphenating with his last name), or by the couple legally declaring a new last name that is sometimes a combination of their two names. Whatever the decision and accompanying rationale, the argument seems to rest on the value attached to names and the weight ascribed to this practice within the context of cultural values around names and identity.

Bodies

Gender is inscribed *on* our bodies in terms of their shape, size, and appearance, and is also performed through how we use and move our bodies in the world. Our culture constructs masculine and feminine bodies in opposition to one another, with feminine bodies expected to be slender, soft, and hairless, and masculine bodies expected to be taller, broader, more muscular, and hairy. One way to explore and reveal how this works is to look at images that deliberately reverse these constructions.

As feminist sociologist Judith Lorber asserts, "Gender is such a familiar part of daily life that it usually takes a deliberate disruption of our expectations of how women and men are supposed to act to pay attention to how it is produced." Among fans of comic books, there are extensive and ongoing conversations about the gendering of comic book characters, with a vibrant feminist critique of the way that female characters are depicted and the storylines they are given. Below is an example of one artist, Aaron Clutter, who draws attention to how gender is constructed in this aspect of popular culture by depicting male superheroes in feminine clothing and poses. Note that the artist has separated out three distinct aspects of the social construction of gendered bodies: (1) the bodies themselves, in terms of their size and muscularity; (2) the clothing; and (3) bodily posture/presentation. The bodies themselves are still coded masculine, with broad shoulders, square jaws, and defined, bulging muscles, but the clothing and poses are distinctly feminine and sexualized.

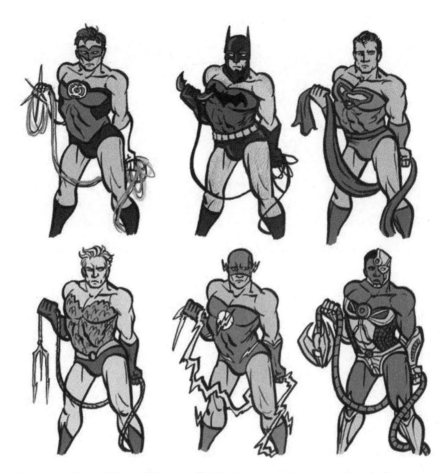

Figure 2.5 Aaron Clutter, Editor-in-Chief, *Comic Booked*, www.comicbooked.com

Artist Hana Pesut's photographic series entitled "Switcheroo" explores similar terrain. The series consists of paired, side-by-side photographs; in the first, a couple poses together wearing their own clothing, whereas in the second the couple switches places and clothing, and also recreates the other's pose and posture.

In this example, we get a visual reminder and confirmation that in some ways, the boundaries of femininity are more elastic than the boundaries of masculinity when it comes to clothing. When the women in these photographs swap the clothes previously worn by the man, they are often oversized but not necessarily categorically different

Figure 2.6 "'Switcheroo' Photography by Hana Pesut," www.sincerelyhana.com

than clothing we would recognize as commonly seen worn by women, whereas the reverse is much less often true for the men in the photographs. At the same time, however, the postures and poses are often quite different, such that seeing the women mimic the men's posture and pose and vice versa is startling and upsets expectations. Feminist philosopher Sandra Bartky has explored these gender differences in "gesture, posture, movement, and general bodily comportment," noting that "Feminine movement, gesture, and posture must exhibit not only constriction, but grace and a certain eroticism restrained by modesty: all three" (451). Henley and Freeman's early work in this area explores similar territory; they note that "It is often considered 'unladylike' for a woman to use her body too forcefully, to sprawl, to stand with her legs widely spread, to sit with her feet up, or to cross the ankle of one leg over the knee of the other. Many of these positions are ones of strength and dominance" (83). They further note that differences in masculine and feminine clothing styles help reinforce these differences, as masculine clothing allows greater range of motion and more coverage. Bartky makes a similar point when noting that "women in short, low-cut dresses are told to avoid bending over at all, but if they must, great care must be taken to avoid an unseemly display of breast or rump" (83). While the increasing sexualization of women's bodies has meant that there are, for better or worse, fewer restrictions on exposing bare skin, we can see evidence of the continuation of this gender norm on websites devoted to celebrity gossip and entertainment "news"; these sites delight in posting paparazzi photos of so-called wardrobe malfunctions or inadvertent flashing, both to titillate viewers but also to subtly or not-so-subtly shame said celebrities for lapses in ladylike presentation.

Yet another way that gender is inscribed on the body is through tattooing. The global history of tattooing is long and complex, and social norms related to tattoos have changed considerably in the past few decades. While historically it was considered to be a significant transgression of feminine gender norms for women to be tattooed, the norms are much more nuanced today, and there is no longer a significant gap between the number of men and women who get tattooed. Hawkes, Senn, and Thorn (2004) cite a study that estimates that "women currently acquire half of all tattoos, a rate that has quadrupled since the 1970s" (594). In spite of the relatively equal numbers of men and women getting tattooed, however, studies seem to suggest that there are gendered differences in perceptions of tattooed people.

In order to get at the nuanced ways that tattoos inscribe gender on the body, we need to consider a number of factors, including the placement, type, and size of those tattoos, as well as the race/ethnicity and social class of tattooed women. As we consider each of these factors, we are reminded of how women's bodies are a central site of social negotiation and struggle. On the one hand, many women get tattooed as a way to deliberately reject normative constructions of femininity, whereas other women do so with deliberate and conscious attention toward staying within the bounds of gendered social expectation. With regard to placement, there is first the question of whether a tattoo is visible or generally hidden from view while wearing clothing. Hawkes, Senn, and Thorne's (2004) study found that both men and women had a more negative attitude toward women whose tattoos were visible. For some women, this is precisely the point; they aim to defy expectations of feminine appearance. Beyond visible versus hidden, however, is the question of where on the body the tattoo is placed.

Some parts of the body are particularly laden with meaning when it comes to both gender and sexuality. Many young women get tattooed on the small of their back; in slang terms, these tattoos are frequently called "tramp stamps," language that is both gendered and sexualized, in that it is an aspect of **slut shaming**. Arguably, there are also classed associations with the "tramp stamp" label. A tattoo in that location is often described as "trashy," as opposed to respectably middle-class. Research shows that the size of a woman's tattoo is also a factor in whether and to what extent it is seen as a violation of feminine gender norms, with smaller tattoos being seen as more feminine than larger ones. Color and type are also important factors; pastel or primary-colored tattoos of butterflies, hearts, roses, the names or footprints/handprints of children, and inspirational words or phrases, are all generally considered feminine.

A final point here is that the consumer marketplace has responded to women's desire to navigate this tricky gender landscape and perhaps to try to have it both ways, so to speak, as evidenced by the cosmetic company Sephora's tattoo concealer makeup, which carries the name of Kat Von D, celebrity tattoo artist, star of reality television show *LA Ink*, herself heavily tattooed. From the Sephora website: "Kat says, 'If you wanna hide a tattoo just for one day, the proper concealer can make that happen! No one has to see what you don't want them to see!' Take it from the tattoo pro: 'I think just as much as people have the choice to be tattooed, they should also have the liberty to look whatever way they want whenever they want.' This is your ticket to tattoo freedom!"

Case Study

The History of Clerical Work and the Secretarial Profession: In today's labor force, clerical work generally and secretary or receptionist positions specifically are female dominated; however, clerical work up through the late 19th century was an exclusively male profession. As England notes, prior to the 20th century, few women engaged in paid work; less than one-fifth of women worked outside the home, and they were typically employed in the areas of domestic work, agriculture, and factory work (particularly textiles). In 1871, according to Boyer, "clerical work accounted for a tiny proportion of all workers, less than one percent in the US in 1870 and Canada in 1871. Clerical work in the US grew by over 450 percent between 1900 and 1903, at which point 9 percent of the labor force held clerical jobs" (310). Workers performing clerical functions were almost exclusively male, and the clerical occupation was "high status work, offered good job security and for those men in senior positions was a most prestigious job of the sort associated with middle management today" (310). The International Association of Administrative Professionals describes the historical roots of secretarial work as far back as Rome up through the Renaissance and late 19th century, when secretarial and clerical duties were predominated by men who "maintained account books, in addition to performing stenographic duties, and were known for their exemplary penmanship skills" (International Association).

With the development of technologies like typewriters and stenography, in 1880, cultural attitudes about women's stereotypical traits like compliance and fine motor coordination/dexterity led to occupational shifts, although these were visions of femininity typically connected to white women; over time (through various media imagery and advertising campaigns, an increase in demand for clerical workers that accompanied technological and industrial shifts from agricultural to urban industries), the demand and rewards for this type of work changed. England notes, "In the popular imaginary, clerical work was promoted as a desirable job for young, educated white women to do for a few years prior to marriage" (313); race and ethnic bias accompanied this shift as office work was believed to be "reserved only for young, white protestant women" (314). Feminist scholars have examined the way that secretarial work offered some women opportunities to enter the labor market, while simultaneously positioning the work as low status, even as the technology aptitude and literacy required to do the work effectively was high. For example, Liz Rohan has challenged the class bias that has framed salaried professional work as higher skilled than the hourly wage work done by secretaries and clerical staff, even when the "amount of technological skill [and] . . . the amount of training and literacy the secretaries need to proofread technical documents" is substantial (Rohan 242).

In today's economy, secretarial work is almost exclusively performed by women and yet the tasks associated with this occupation have not substantially changed. This shift highlights how, in this case, economic forces and cultural shifts substantially changed an occupation assumed to be high status and requiring traditional masculine traits to one that has become dramatically female dominated with no accompanying change in duties, highlighting the way that social institutions can shift and adapt our understanding of gender over time.

End of Chapter Elements

Evaluating Prior Knowledge

1. Think about your own exposure to gender identity and gender awareness. Do you remember when you first became aware (or were made aware) of your gender? What moment or moments in your life have you experienced a sense of what it means to be a boy or a girl? What cues did you get that led you to that awareness? How was your awareness of your gender intertwined with other aspects of your identity, such as you social class, your race/ethnicity, and/or your sexual identity?

2. Have there been moments in your life that you've felt limited or empowered by your gender identity? In what settings did you have those experiences?

3. This chapter briefly discusses several of the sites or arenas where gender socialization takes place. What do you recall about your experiences with those institutions when you were growing up? And today?

Application Exercises

1. Occupational segregation by gender is one explanation for the gender pay gap. See Figure 2, 4, which documents the occupational segregation of labor, and examine the dominance of each gender in particular occupations. Select one female-dominated field and explain what qualities are typically associated with the responsibilities of that work environment. Do the same for a male-dominated

occupation. How might a biological determinist explain this occupational clustering? What would a social constructionist focus on?

2. Choose a favorite film genre and screen at least three films in that genre. Take note of the number and type of women characters and relevant identity factors—marital status, educational attainment, race, class, **sexual orientation**. What conclusions can you draw about "women in X genre" of film based on your analysis? What messages about gender would you draw as a viewer just paying attention to norms, values, and behaviors exhibited by female characters in that genre?

3. Take a field trip to a local department store like Wal-Mart or Target and peruse the toy aisles. Jot down what you observe about the messages, implications, and subtext communicated by the arrangement of the toys; how they are divided, marketed, packaged, and directed; and what they communicate about gender.

4. Select a popular teen magazine—*Seventeen*, *YM*, *Teen*, *Teen Vogue*— and examine the representation of menstruation, feminine hygiene products, and sexuality. What observations can you make about the marketing, messaging, rhetoric, and imagery associated with menstruation? Is it addressed in ads or feature stories? What conclusions can you draw about cultural messaging around menstruation?

Skills Assessment/Check for Understanding

1. In your own words, summarize the central emphasis of each of three approaches to gender systems: **biological determinism**, psychodynamic and developmental, and social constructionist.

2. View the 2013 film *Gravity*, paying careful attention to the gendered identities of the two main characters, played by Sandra Bullock and George Clooney. In what ways does each behave in "gender-normed" ways? In what ways does each defy them?

3. Two of the academic fields with the smallest percentage of women earning doctorates are engineering[7] (22%) and philosophy[8] (21.9%). Explore your impressions and associations with these two fields of academic study; are they "gendered masculine" in ways that explain this disparity? If so, are they gendered masculine in similar or different ways?

Discussion Questions

1. Why do you think that biological explanations for gender roles and expectations are so powerful and common sense? In what ways do biological explanations fail to account for human experiences broadly or your own experience specifically?

2. In what ways can you observe race, class, and sexuality operating in definitions of masculinity and femininity?

3. Prior to reading this chapter, had you ever encountered the word "cisgender" or "cissexual"? If so, where? If you had not encountered these terms before, what do you make of them? If you identify as cisgender, how does it feel to have a label to describe that identity?

Writing Prompts

1. Describe a gender norm that you regularly perform and that, for the purposes of this assignment, you are willing to break for a set period of time. Describe how you broke the norm and who saw you break it. What reactions did you receive? How does your experiment support and/or challenge the arguments contained in this chapter? How does your experiment illustrate this chapter's key concepts?

2. Screen the documentary *Tough Guise 2: Violence, Manhood, and American Culture* or *The Bro Code: How Contemporary Culture Creates Sexist Men*. Then do some Internet research into the school shootings that most traumatized Americans: the Columbine shooting in 1999 and the Newtown shootings in 2012. Write an essay in which you examine the phenomenon of school shootings through a social constructionist lens that considers the formation of masculine identities in the United States.

3. Select two of the following comedic films targeting young male viewers. What vision of masculinity do they construct? *Van Wilder, Old School, Pineapple Express, Caddyshack, The Big Lebowski, Tropic Thunder, The Royal Tenenbaums, Swingers, Harold and Kumar Go to White Castle.*

4. Take a brief tour through a department store or big box store like Target or Wal-Mart (or their websites), looking carefully at the newborn, baby, and toddler sections of clothing and accessories

(e.g., bibs and pacifiers). Make a list of all the gendered messages that are communicated through text, images, colors, styles, and so forth. What conclusions can you draw about how gender is "framed" even as early as infancy? What qualities, activities, and characteristics are emphasized for girls versus boys?

Notes

1   www.babble.com/baby/boy-or-girl-4-month-old-being-raised-genderless/
2   https://in.news.yahoo.com/couple-finally-reveals-child-s-gender--five-years-after-birth-20120123.html
3   www.womensmediacenter.com/blog/entry/rape-joke-supercut-i-cant-believe-you-clapped-for-that
4   www.thenation.com/blog/168856/anatomy-successful-rape-joke
5   http://kateharding.info/2012/07/13/15-rape-jokes-that-work/
6   http://jezebel.com/5925186/how-to-make-a-rape-joke
7   www.insidehighered.com/news/2010/09/14/doctorates#sthash.1uZBi8e6.dpbs
8   http://opinionator.blogs.nytimes.com/2013/09/02/women-in-philosophy-do-the-math/?_php=true&_type=blogs&_php=true&_type=blogs&_php=true&_type=blogs&_r=2&

Works Cited and Suggested Readings

Angier, Natalie. *Woman: An Intimate Geography.* New York: Anchor, 2000. Print.

Bartky, Sandra. "Foucault, Femininity, and the Modernization of Patriarchal Power." *The Politics of Women's Bodies: Sexuality, Appearance, and Behavior.* Ed. Rose Weitz. 3rd edition. New York: Oxford UP, 2010. 76–97. Print.

Bettis, Pamela, and Natalie Guice Adams. "Short Skirts and Breast Juts: Cheerleading, Eroticism, and Schools." *Sex Education.* 6.2 (May 2006): 121–133. Print.

Bielanko, Monica. "Boy or Girl? 4-Month-Old Being Raised Genderless." Shine at Yahoo. 24 May 2011. Web.

Bordo, Susan. *Unbearable Weight: Feminism, Western Culture, and the Body.* Berkeley: U of California P, 1993. Print.

Bornstein, Kate. *Gender Outlaw: On Men, Women, and the Rest of Us.* Vintage: New York, 1995. Print.

Brinton, Mary. "Gendered Offices: A Comparative-Historical Examination of Clerical Work in Japan and the United States." Stanford: Stanford UP, 2007. 87–111. Print.

Brumberg, Joan Jacobs. *The Body Project: An Intimate History of American Girls.* New York: Vintage Books, 1997. Print.

Butler, Judith. *Gender Trouble: Feminism and the Subversion of Identity.* New York: Routledge, 1990. Print.

Center for American Women and Politics. Rutgers University. 25 May 2014. Web.

"Couple Finally Reveals Child's Gender, Five Years After Birth." Yahoo Shine. January 2012. Web.

Crittenden, Ann. *The Price of Motherhood: Why the Most Important Job in the World Is Still the Least Valued.* New York, Picador P, 2010. Print.

Davis, Angela Y. *Women, Race, and Class*. New York: Vintage, 1983. Print.

Department of Labor. "Highlights of Women's Earning in 2010." Bureau of Labor Statistics. July 2011. Web.

Diehm, Jan, and Margaret Wheeler Johnson. "Gender Wage Gap Heavily Influenced by Occupation Segregation." *Huffington Post*. 11 June 2013. Web.

Duberman, Amanda. "Why Women CEOs Are Fired More Than Men." *Huffington Post*. 7 May 2014. Web.

Dusenbery, Maya. "Why the Gender Gap in Children's Allowances Matters." *Feministing*. 24 April 2014. Web.

England, Kim, and Kate Boyer. "Women's Work: The Feminization and Shifting Meanings of Clerical Work. *Journal of Social History*. 43.2 (Winter 2009): 307–340. Web.

Fausto-Sterling, Anne. *Sexing the Body*. New York: Basic Books, 2000. Print.

——. *Sex/Gender: Biology in a Social World*. New York: Routledge, 2012. Print.

Fortini, Amanda. "The 'Bitch' and the 'Ditz.'" *New York*. 16 November 2008. Web.

Gabriel, Paul, and Susanne Schmitz. "Gender Differences in Occupational Distributions among Workers." *Monthly Labor Review*. June 2007. 19–24. Web.

Girl Scouts of America. "Frequently Asked Questions: Social Issues." 28 May 2014. Web.

Gould, Lois. "X: A Fabulous Child's Story." Article appeared in *Polare* magazine: February 1998. Last Update: June 2013. Web.

Grose, Jessica. "Cleaning: The Final Feminist Frontier." *New Republic*. 19 March 2013. Web.

Halberstam, Judith. *Female Masculinity*. Durham, NC: Duke UP, 1998. Print.

Halper, Katie. "How to Win a Best Actress Oscar." *Feministing*. 21 January 2014. Web.

Harris, Lynn. "Mrs. Feminist." *Salon*. 14 October 2003. Web.

Hawkes, Daina, Charlene Y. Senn, and Chantal Thorn. "Factors that Influence Attitudes Toward Women with Tattoos." *Sex Roles*. 50 (May 2004): 593–604. Print.

Henley, Nancy and Jo Freeman. "The Sexual Politics of Interpersonal Behavior." *Women: Images and Realities*. Ed. Suzanne Kelly, Gowri Parameswaran, and Nancy Schniedewind. 5th edition. New York: McGraw Hill, 2012. 82–88. Print.

Henn, Steve. "Facebook Gives Users New Options to Identify Gender." *All Tech Considered*. National Public Radio. 13 February 2014. Web.

Hetter, Katia. "Girl Scouts Accepts Transgender Kid, Provokes Cookie Boycott." *CNN*. 13 January 2012. Web.

Hlavka, Heather. "Normalizing Sexual Violence: Young Women Account for Harassment and Abuse." *Gender and Society*. 28 February 2014. Web.

hooks, bell. *Feminism Is for Everybody: Passionate Politics*. London: Pluto P, 2000. Print.

"Hours Spend Doing Unpaid Household Work by Age and Sex, 2003–2007." Bureau of Labor Statistics. 6 August 2009. Web.

Hurt, Byron. "Why I Am a Male Feminist." *The Root*. 16 March 2011. Web.

Ingraham, Chrys. *White Weddings: Romancing Heterosexuality in Popular Culture*. New York: Routledge, 1999. Print.

International Association of Administrative Professionals. "History of Secretarial Profession." *International Association of Administrative Professionals*. 2010. Web.

International Cheer Union. "History of Cheerleading." 24 February 2014. Web.

Johnson, Allan. *The Gender Knot: Unraveling Our Patriarchal Legacy*. Philadelphia: Temple UP, 1997. Print.

Johnson, Jenna. "On College Campuses, a Gender Gap in Student Government." *The Washington Post*. 16 March 2011. Web.

Junior Achievement USA and the Allstate Foundation Teens and Personal Finance Survey. 10 April 2014. Web.

Kawashima-Ginsberg, Kei, and Nancy Thomas. "Civic Engagement and Political Leadership Among Women—A Call for Solutions." CIRCLE Fact Sheet. May 2013. Web.

Kimmel, Michael. *Manhood in America: A Cultural History*. 3rd edition. New York: Oxford UP, 2011.

Kivel, Paul. "The 'Act-Like-A-Man' Box." *Men's Lives*. 7th ed. Ed. Michael S. Kimmel and Michael A. Messner. Boston: Pearson, 2007. 148–150. Print.

Lockwood, Penelope, Caitlin Burton, and Katelyn Boersma. "Tampering with Tradition: Rationales Concerning Women's Married Names and Children's Surnames." *Sex Roles*. 65 (2011): 827–839. Web.

Lorber, Judith. *Paradoxes of Gender*. New Haven: Yale UP, 1994. Print.

Lorde, Audre. *Zami: A New Spelling of My Name: A Biomythography*. Freedom, CA: Crossing P, 1997. Print.

McDonough, Katie. "Report: Many Girls View Sexual Assault as Normal Behavior." *Salon*. 14 April 2014. Web.

McKinnon, Catherine. *Toward a Feminist Theory of the State*. Cambridge: Harvard UP, 1989. Print.

Mifflin, Margot. *Bodies of Subversion: A Secret History of Women and Tattoo*. 3rd edition. New York: powerHouse Books. 2013. Print.

Milkman, Katherine, Modupe Akinola, and Dolly Chugh. "What Happens Before? A Field Experiment Exploring How Pay and Representation Differentially Shape Bias on the Pathway into Organizations." *Social Science Research Network*. 23 April 2014. Web.

Mills, C. Wright. *The Sociological Imagination*. New York: Oxford UP, 1959. Print.

Moss-Racusin, Corrine, John F. Dovidio, Victoria L. Brescoll, Mark J. Graham, and Jo Handelsman. "Science Faculty's Subtle Gender Biases Favor Male Students." *PNAS*. 109 (41): 16474–16479. Print.

Pesut, Hana. *Switcheroo*. Minneapolis: Schapco, 2013. Print.

Rich, Adrienne. "Compulsory Heterosexuality and Lesbian Existence." *Blood, Bread, and Poetry: Selected Prose, 1979–1985*. New York: Norton, 1986. 23–75. Print.

Richardson, Sarah. "Y All the Hype?" *Slate.com*. 5 May 2014. Web.

Rohan, Liz. "Reveal Codes: A New Lens for Examining and Historicizing the Work of Secretaries." *Computers and Composition*. 20.3 (2003): 237–253. Print.

Rotella, Elyce. "The Transformation of the American Office: Changes in Employment and Technology." *Journal of Economic History*. 41.1 (March 1981): 51–57. Print.

Sadker, David, and Karen R. Zittleman. "Gender Inequity in School: Not a Thing of the Past." Women: Images and Realities, A Multicultural Anthology. Ed. Amy Kesselman, Lily D. McNair and Nancy Schniedewind. New York: McGraw Hill, 2011. Print.

Scheuble, Laurie, David R. Johnson, and Katherine M. Johnson. "Marital Name Changing Attitudes and Plans of College Students: Comparing Change over Time and across Regions." *Sex Roles*. 66 (2012): 282–292. Web.

Seelye, Katharine Q. "School Vote Stirs Debate on Girls as Leaders." *New York Times*. 11 April 2013. Web.

Sharp, Gwen. "We Like You a Lot, Ms. Scientist, But We'd Rather Hire the Guy." Weblog entry. *Ms. Magazine Blog*. 26 September 2012. Web.

Stryker, Susan. *Transgender History*. Berkeley, CA: Seal P, 2008. Print.

Thomas, Katie. "Born on Sideline, Cheering Clamors to be a Sport." *New York Times*. 22 May 2011. Web.

Wade, Lisa. "American Men's Hidden Crisis: They Need More Friends!" *Slate*. 7 December 2013. Web.

Weil, Elizabeth. "What if It's (Sort of) a Boy and (Sort of) a Girl?" *NYTimes.com*. 24 September 2006. Web.

Williams, Joan, and Rachel Dempsey. *What Works for Women at Work: Four Patterns Working Women Need to Know*. Albany: NYUP, 2014. Print.

Yoder, Brian. "Engineering by the Numbers." American Society for Engineering Education. 2011–2012. Web.

Yogachandra, Natascha. "Teaching Positive Masculinity." *Atlantic*. 14 May 2014. Web.

3

PRIVILEGE AND OPPRESSION

Figure 3.1 Getty Images/*Boston Globe*

Opening Illustration

In 1967, the idea of women participating in a long-distance race as
grueling as the Boston Marathon was so farfetched that no official
document stated that women were prohibited. Kathrine Switzer, a

19-year old Syracuse student, loved running and had been training with her coach Arnie Briggs to do long-distance races; she even completed a 30-miler to prepare herself to complete in the flagship race in the United States. Registering as K.V. Switzer, Kathrine started the race with Briggs and her boyfriend, Tom Miller. Two miles in, race officials attempted to eject her from the race, with race director Jock Semple lunging at her, attempting to pull her from the course and tear off her race number (see Figure 3.1). Miller and Briggs deflected Semple, allowing Kathrine to finish the 26.2 mile race in a respectable 4 hours and 20 minutes. The experience was a life-changing one for Switzer, as her experience inspired her to become a lifelong advocate for equal opportunity for women in athletics and beyond. More broadly, Switzer's historic run helped propel a sea change in women's sports, marked in 1972 by women's official inclusion in the Boston Marathon and the passage of Title IX legislation, which prohibited discrimination in education, including athletic programs. Change came a bit more slowly to the Olympics, however; it was not until 1984 that the women's marathon was first included as an event.

We open the chapter with this story because it illustrates the chapter's threshold concepts, privilege and oppression, particularly institutional structures that shape our individual experiences, and how activism, agency, and advocacy—as well as the action of feminist allies—can challenge and ultimately change those structures. As you read this chapter, consider how the key concepts outlined are at work in Switzer's historical action as part of completing the end-of-chapter Application Exercise.

A *feminist stance* posits that systems of privilege and oppression profoundly shape individual lives. These systems play out via **ideology** and societal institutions and are internalized by individuals.

Why a Threshold Concept?

Now that you have started to develop an understanding of the concept of a socially constructed sex/gender system, the next step is to broaden our inquiry, or widen our lens, to use a visual metaphor. Imagine a film that opens with a close-up shot and then quickly pans out to show the viewer the bigger picture. That's precisely the move we'll be making in this chapter. Although we began this textbook by focusing on the power dynamics that are at play in the gender system, when we widen our lens we are able to see that similar dynamics structure many other systems of difference and inequality. Sexism, the system of oppression and privilege based in gender, is but one type of oppression. What's more, these additional structures of oppression and privilege are interconnected and mutually reinforcing (a point that will be developed more fully in Chapter 4 on intersectionality).

Definitions: Privilege and Oppression

The concepts of privilege and oppression provide a fundamental framework for understanding how power operates in society. This framework helps explain people's experiences in the world, and it provides us with tools to name and describe our social location. *Oppression* can be defined as prejudice and discrimination directed toward a group and perpetuated by the ideologies and practices of multiple social institutions. A number of scholars and activists have explored the ways of thinking and the mechanisms through which these systems are created and perpetuated. For example, legal scholar Mari Matsuda notes that "All forms of oppression involve taking a trait X, which often carries with it a cultural meaning, and using X to make some group the 'other' and to reduce their entitlements and power." This terminology of privilege and oppression, then, gives us the tools to name and describe not just sexism but the whole "-ism family," as Gloria Yamato calls it; for example, **racism**, **classism**, **heterosexism**, and **ableism**.

Within each system of privilege and oppression, we can see that there is a dominant group and a marginalized group, one group who is considered to be the norm, with their counterpart being the "other." Audre Lorde calls it a **mythical norm**, "usually defined as white, thin, male, young, heterosexual, christian, and financially secure," and goes on to argue that "It is with this mythical norm that the trappings of power reside within this society" (116). Those who are outside the mythical norm in one or more ways are seen as lesser as a result of being judged in relation to it. As discussed in Chapter 2, masculinity is the default norm in our culture, and it is valued more highly than femininity. The same can be said for being able-bodied, young, white, and so forth. Audre Lorde argues that "we have *all* been programmed to respond to the human differences between us with fear and loathing and to handle that difference in one of three ways: ignore it, and if that is not possible, copy it if we think it is dominant, or destroy it if we think it is subordinate" (115). As we will discuss in this chapter, idealization of the mythical norm manifests in many ways, both material and ideological.

In addition to the scholarship that has explored the ways of thinking that create and perpetuate systems of privilege and oppression, many scholars have also explored in depth how these systems manifest, that is, what forms they take. Oppression can take *cultural and symbolic* forms (discussed in the "Ideologies" section), such as images of beauty and success, and *material* forms (discussed in the "Institutions" section), such as structured forms of failure that disproportionately impact some groups more than others.

For members of marginalized groups, as Marilyn Frye notes, the experience is "that the living of one's life is confined and shaped by forces and barriers which are not accidental or occasional and hence avoidable, but are systematically related to each other in such a way as to catch one between and among them and restrict or penalize motion in any direction" (43). Labeling one's experience with oppression, framed through the "wide lens" that we describe previously, means using the sociological imagination discussed in Chapter 2, and situating one's experience within a broader framework; often, this means revising a personal understanding of successes, failures, and circumstances from narratives of individual action and personal will to a paradigm that considers how those experiences fit in with social, material, and economic forces.

On the flip side, *privilege* can be defined as benefits, advantages, and power that accrue to members of a dominant group as a result of the oppression of the marginalized group; individuals and groups may be privileged without realizing, recognizing, or even wanting it. Antiracist activist Tim Wise has used his own experience with white privilege and the historical and cultural factors that define his social location to illustrate the concept of white, male privilege. Wise argues that "to be white [in the US] not only means that one will typically inherit certain advantages from the past but also means that one will continue to reap the benefits of ongoing racial privilege, which itself is the flipside of discrimination against persons of color," (xi). Here he details the historical and legal circumstances of his family that ultimately allowed him, as a white man, to benefit from those injustices and advance socially and educationally. For example, as the child of a middle-income household with relatively modest standardized test scores, Wise found himself a not particularly competitive applicant to the selective Tulane University. Wise traces back his mother's ability (even as a woman who had never owned a piece of property) to take out a loan to help him pay tuition, with his grandmother as a cosigner. His grandmother also had never worked outside the home, and her ability to cosign was inextricably linked to her marriage to a white man whose financial fortunes rested on his racial whiteness—working in the military and government in an era when people of color were systematically denied such opportunities, and buying a house in a neighborhood where, due to a lack of legal structures to prevent housing discrimination, people of color did not live (Wise 12–13). As Wise concludes, "Although not every white person's story is the same as mine, the simple truth is that any white person born before 1964, at least, was legally elevated above any person of color, and as such received directly the privileges, the head start, the advantages of whiteness as a matter of course" (13). A key point here is that oppression and privilege are inextricably linked; they are opposite sides of the same coin. For every type of oppression, a corresponding set of privileges exist. That is, the flip side of sexism is male privilege; of racism, white privilege; of heterosexism, heterosexual privilege, and so forth.

One of the best known essays on the topic of white privilege is Peggy Mcintosh's "White Privilege: Unpacking the Invisible Knapsack," where she writes: "I was taught to see racism only in individual acts of meanness, not in invisible systems conferring dominance on my group" and "I have come to see white privilege as an invisible package of unearned assets that I can count on cashing in each day, but about which I was "meant" to remain oblivious. White privilege is like an invisible weightless knapsack of special provisions, maps, passports, codebooks, visas, clothes, tools, and blank checks." Mcintosh's essay is now a classic because of its trenchant enumeration of all the (most unconscious) assumptions that white people make on a day-to-day basis about their social location and role in the world. Some of the clearest include her notes on "Daily Effects of White Privilege":

7. When I am told about our national heritage or about "civilization," I am shown that people of my color made it what it is.

8. I can be sure that my children will be given curricular materials that testify to the existence of their race.

13. Whether I use checks, credit cards or cash, I can count on my skin color not to work against the appearance of financial reliability.

16. I can be pretty sure that my children's teachers and employers will tolerate them if they fit school and workplace norms; my chief worries about them do not concern others' attitudes toward their race.

20. I can do well in a challenging situation without being called a credit to my race.

21. I am never asked to speak for all the people of my racial group.

22. I can remain oblivious of the language and customs of persons of color who constitute the world's majority without feeling in my culture any penalty for such oblivion.

25. If a traffic cop pulls me over or if the IRS audits my tax return, I can be sure I haven't been singled out because of my race.

34. I can worry about racism without being seen as self-interested or self-seeking.

36. If my day, week or year is going badly, I need not ask of each negative episode or situation whether it had racial overtones.

46. I can chose blemish cover or bandages in "flesh" color and have them more or less match my skin.

What Mcintosh's ideas call attention to are the specific ways that privilege operates in daily life. She argues that, although whites may have experiences that feel like discrimination, those experiences are generally not attributable to their racial identity. Further, McIntosh's examples show individual experience within the context of larger structures and institutions: law enforcement, government agencies, educational institutions, and so forth.

In order to fully understand these concepts, however, we have to be willing to think on a "macro level," which is not particularly easy to do. In our experiences of talking about and teaching these concepts, we have found that some misconceptions and misunderstandings crop up over and over again. We detail a few of them in this chapter.

Learning Roadblock

"You keep using that word. I do not think it means what you think it means." Research on learning has shown that a learner's existing understanding strongly influences how that learner absorbs new information. The use of "privilege" in this discipline-specific context requires some rethinking of the commonsense use of the term "privilege," or the way we refer to it in everyday life. Most frequently, we think of a privilege as something like a "gift" or "honor," an opportunity of some kind. What differentiates privilege as a kind of term used in Women's and Gender Studies is the notion that privilege refers not just to individual opportunity but to structured and social opportunities, particularly those that are systematically granted on the basis of a social category of identity rather than merit or individual will.

But it's not just that our commonsense understanding of privilege gets in the way of grasping how we use that term here. Another more fundamental kind of misunderstanding can come from the fact that this framework of privilege and oppression runs counter to the values and assumptions of many people in our culture. A recent example that was in the news can help illustrate this point.

At Delavan-Darien High School in Wisconsin, a parent complained about a teacher's use of materials on white privilege in an "American Diversity" course. After looking at the course materials, which drew on the work of Tim Wise and Peggy McIntosh, the parent drew the conclusion that the materials were divisive, and that they had the intention of inducing "white guilt." It seems clear that the parent rejected the overall premise that society is structured into systems of oppression and privilege, and she was quoted as saying that, in her understanding of them, the course materials were saying "If you're white, you're oppressing. If you're non white, you've been a victim." The parent seems to be thinking only in individual terms, as opposed to structural, macro-level terms. Michael Kimmel, a sociologist who has written extensively about privilege, argues that statements like these "are as revealing as they are irrelevant." He notes the strong impulse in our culture to "individualize and personalize processes that are social and structural" (2), and goes on to point out that this type of response is a way to dodge and avoid taking these issues seriously.

Institutions

In Chapter 2, we introduced the concept of gender socialization. As a part of that discussion, we asked you to consider both where and how we are socialized into our gender, that is, where we learn what it means to be a boy or a girl, a man or a woman, in our society. Those sites of gender socialization are our society's institutions, and as we mentioned there, they consist of marriage, family, the educational system, the health care system, religion, mass media, the military, the political system, the legal and criminal justice systems, sports, and the economy. We return to a discussion of institutions in the context of this chapter on oppression and privilege because systems of oppression and privilege are embedded within and are played out through these societal institutions.

In Chapter 2, we focused on how societal institutions are patriarchal in nature; that is, as Allan Johnson explains, male-dominated, male-identified, male-centered, and obsessed with control, particularly of women. Here we go one step further by stating that (1) societal institutions also structure oppression and privilege based on race, class, and sexual identity, as well as other categories of identity; and (2) that these systems of oppression and privilege overlap with and reinforce one another. In other words, these systems cannot be understood in isolation from one another.

The term "institutions" and "institutional or structural" forms of oppression are used frequently to highlight the way that systems function to grant resources and privileges to some groups and withhold them from others. Institutions can be formal, organized structures like law and policy–making groups (the House of Representatives and

Senate, the Food and Drug Administration, or the medical profession and its related professional organizations), or they can be less formal but still an agreed-upon way of organizing and reproducing social norms (e.g., mass media and popular culture). In other ways, institutions can have a combination of formal and informal structural elements. For example, "marriage" as an institution is governed by formal laws that dictate who can marry and under what conditions; it is simultaneously shaped by formal religious organizations that grant benefits to certain couples and not others, and that enact doctrine that participants in that faith are expected to comply with in order to remain in good standing. Simultaneously, social norms about marriage are promulgated via other informal institutions such as mass media and other aspects of popular culture (think, for example, of the number of magazines, television shows, and websites that are devoted to wedding culture). The example of marriage also illustrates the points made in the previous paragraph, in that not only is the institution of marriage historically patriarchal but also heterosexist. And in the 21st century, marriage is increasingly becoming a middle-class institution that consolidates and protects the privileges of those with economic means and serves to further marginalize working-class and poor people.

Misconception Alert

Racism, sexism, and other forms of oppression happen only on an individual level. One of the most challenging concepts to understand in many sociologically based disciplines and in Women's and Gender Studies specifically are the differences between what feminist scholar Beverly Daniel Tatum identifies as bigotry, prejudice, and racism. It's important to distinguish between these three ideas because whereas the first two happen on a practical and potentially individual level, the last is systemic. As with patriarchy, racism is not the product or conduct of an individual person but what Tatum defines as "a system involving cultural messages and institutional policies and practices as well as the beliefs and actions of individuals" (362). Some people use "prejudice" and "bigotry" as interchangeable with "racism"; bigotry is a personal belief system that may manifest in acts of meanness or hostility on an individual level. Prejudice is a preconception about an individual on the basis of a racial identity. Racism differs from either of these because it involves what David Wellman has called a "system of advantage based on race" and means prejudice plus bigotry plus power, or the ability to grant privileges to groups and withhold them from others.

The critical elements differentiating oppression from simple prejudice and discrimination are that it is a group phenomenon and that institutional power and authority are used to support prejudices and enforce discriminatory behaviors in systematic ways. Everyone is socialized to participate in oppressive practices, either as direct and indirect perpetrators or passive beneficiaries, or—as with some oppressed peoples—by directing discriminatory behaviors at members of one's own group.

Ideologies

The concept of ideology might be one that you have heard before, as academics tend to use it *a lot*, but you might not really know what it means or why it's used so much. We are introducing it in the context of this chapter on privilege and oppression, along with institutions, because it is the other primary means or method through which those systems of oppression and privilege manifest and are played out.

Quite simply, ideologies are sets of ideas or beliefs. Just as there are dominant and marginalized groups in society, so there are dominant ideologies. Ideologies always represent the attitudes, interests, and values of a particular group. Lynn Weber defines dominant ideologies as "pervasive societal beliefs that reflect the dominant culture's vision about what is right and proper. Controlling images (stereotypes) are dominant-culture ideologies about subordinate groups that serve to restrict their options, to constrain them" (117). Literary critic Terry Eagleton has defined ideology as "those modes of feeling, valuing, perceiving, and believing which have some kind of relation to the maintenance and reproduction of social power" (15). And Mari Matsuda asserts that "Language, including the language of science, law, rights, necessity, free markets, neutrality, and objectivity can make subordination seem natural and inevitable, justifying material deprivation" (336). What we invite you to do is to develop a heightened awareness of the ways that ideologies operate in culture at large as well as in your own life and thinking. This involves developing *metacognition*—or thinking about one's own thinking or thinking processes. Understanding ideologies means being able to (1) identify patterns of thinking, (2) monitor one's own thinking for those patterns of belief, and (3) critically reflect on how one's ideas and attitudes are shaped by those beliefs.

Privilege and oppression play out in the institution of health care in the United States, where the amount and quality of health care people have access to is shaped by economic resources or the lack thereof, as well as racism. The U.S. Department of Health and Human Services Office of Minority Health, for example, has documented significant disparities in the health outcomes of marginalized racial and ethnic groups. Their action plan to reduce health disparities notes, "Individuals, families and communities that have systematically experienced social and economic disadvantage face greater obstacles to optimal health. Characteristics such as race or ethnicity, religion, SES, gender, age, mental health, disability, sexual orientation or gender identity, geographic location, or other characteristics historically linked to exclusion or discrimination are known to influence health status." The report notes that these health disparities are not only about lack of access to care, but about the kind of care that people of color receive when seeking it. More specifically, they note that "Racial and ethnic minorities are more likely than non-Hispanic Whites to report experiencing poorer quality patient-provider interactions." These patient–provider interactions are often of poor quality because providers may bring stereotypical understandings of patients into their treatment. In other words, ideology also plays a role in shaping people's experiences of the institution of health care. We will return to this topic in Chapter 4.

A related example focuses on gender in health care. While women obtain health care in equal if not greater numbers than men, their experiences may be negatively shaped on a number of levels by gender stereotypes. As we discussed in Chapter 2, in a binary sex/gender system, masculinity is associated with the mind and rationality, and femininity with the body and irrationality. These characteristics have made their way into gender stereotypes of women as hysterical, with their physical complaints not being taken seriously by their health care practitioner. As Laurie Edwards notes in "The Gender Gap in Pain," the Institute of Medicine's 2011 report "Relieving Pain in America" "found that not only did women appear to suffer more from pain, but that women's reports of pain were more likely to be dismissed." Instead, Edwards observes, women's pain is often characterized as "'emotional,' 'psychogenic' and therefore 'not real.'"

An extended example can help better explain and explore the role of both institutions and ideology in maintaining systems of privilege and oppression. The **bootstraps myth** is the idea that upward class mobility is not only possible but probable, and that individual will and hard work are the only requisites for moving out of poverty and into the middle class. One of the consequences or implications of this myth is that poor people are then blamed for their continued poverty. Within the logic of the bootstraps myth, if individual will and hard work are the only requisites for moving out of poverty and into the middle class, then poverty can be explained by a *lack* of will and hard work on the part of poor people.

The ideology of upward class mobility has its roots in the long history of the United States as a colony, but was popularized by a series of novels in the 1890s written by Horatio Alger, novels about hard-working boys whose hard work elevated them from a hardscrabble life to one of success and luxury. So-called Cinderella or rags-to-riches stories continue to be popular and have been continually updated over the past century in such movies as *Pretty Woman*, *Maid in Manhattan*, *The Blind Side*, and *Slumdog Millionaire*. Rags-to-riches stories are also a frequent premise of reality television shows. These narratives have the effect of reinforcing belief in the possibility of dramatic upward mobility. This ideology has great explanatory and persuasive power because it builds upon a cultural belief in *self-determination* that resonates with many U.S. residents, the idea that we are each the captain of our own destinies, as it were. However, data on the realities of social mobility demonstrate that, in fact, movement from one class to a higher or lower one, particularly from the lowest rungs of the American economic ladder to a higher one, is uncommon and difficult, as data from a *New York Times* special feature on social class reveal. In covering the topic of "How Class Works," the *New York Times* tracked American families by income quintile (breaking down family income by quintile) and examining how, over time, people in those income brackets moved up or down the "economic ladder."

Table 3.1 Economic Mobility in the U.S.

Top 20%	Of those in the top quintile, 52% remained there a decade later.	Just 5% had dropped to the bottom quintile.
Upper Middle 20%	Those in the upper middle quintile largely remained there, with 30% in the same income bracket.	Seven percent of the upper middle had dropped to the bottom quintile, while 25% had moved up to the top, and 27% had dropped to the middle.
Bottom 20%	Most notably, those who occupied the bottom quintile generally remained there. The same number of bottom 20 percenters remained poor as top 20 percenters remained rich: 52%.	Similarly, just 5% of bottom quintile earners had reached the top 20%, and a small number had reached the upper middle income bracket: 7.5%.

As these data illustrate, social class is fairly immutable; that is, the bottom fifth of the U.S. population in 1988 largely remained in that economic quintile, with relatively few people born into poverty rising up even a single income quintile. The same immutability is demonstrated for those in the top income quintile. In sum, the class a person is born into greatly shapes life experiences and has a huge impact over the life course. Gregory Mantsios puts it even more bluntly: "Class standing, and consequently life chances, are largely determined at birth," a reality that frames our discussion of the institutions and the various experiences of them.

Many questions follow: Why is it that the class structure in the United States is fairly static? And how can we account for the persistence of the belief in widespread class mobility given the data that disproves it? There are many answers to these questions, but one key factor is the societal institution of education, an institution that reinforces privilege and that some can experience as oppressive. We'll start by looking at the relationship between baccalaureate degree attainment and social class. As the chart below shows, income quartile has enormous predictive power in attainment of four-year degrees, and this disparity between fourth-quartile (the poorest) families and first-quartile (the wealthiest) families has grown in the last 40 years. Eighty-two percent of those individuals in the top quartile of the economic spectrum earned

Figure 3.2 Estimated Baccalaureate Degree Attainment by Age 24 by Family Income Quartile, from 1970 to 2012

Tom Mortensen, PEO Newsletter

a four-year degree, a rate that has doubled in the last four decades to result in the majority of wealthy families producing college graduates; by contrast, the very small percentage of degree-earners from the bottom quartile in 1970 (just 6.2%) has barely budged, up to 8.3%; that is, children raised in wealthy households are 10 times as likely to earn a baccalaureate degree—essentially, entrance into stable employment and household security as well as the starting point for most professional occupations—than those from the poorest families (see Figure 3.2).

Further, the profound interrelationship between nearly all measures of academic achievement and **socioeconomic status (SES)** reveal the deep roots of privilege and oppression, particularly how social strata reproduce and maintain inequality despite the efforts of individuals to navigate them—or to transform them. As Rebecca Zwick reports in "Is the SAT a Wealth Test?", the connections between social class and academic achievement are demonstrated by both the major standardized tests, the SAT and ACT. When comparing student achievement of the benchmark score for admission to selective colleges, a combined verbal and math score of 1100 (in 2001), students from high socioeconomic status (SES) were three and a half times more likely to meet the benchmark (32%) compared with low-SES students (9%). The average SAT score for low-income students was 887, according to Zweck's findings, while scores steadily increase, with the average score for students with family income above $100,000 reaching 1126 (307). Research shows a similar gap on the ACT score, as well as many other standard measures of academic achievement including completion of a rigorous, college-preparation curriculum and high school grades. This is largely attributable to the differential access to resources both at home and in their educational systems including variation in teacher preparation (more teachers with advanced training and credentials teach at schools with lower percentages of students receiving free and reduced lunch). In this way, privilege and oppression in the forms of access to the cultural capital that produce social mobility are structured into a system that reproduces itself with each generation.

This is *not* to say that working-class and poverty-class people cannot do well in school, but that their chances of academic success are lower than their more affluent peers. A 2014 *New York Times* story highlights the gap between high-income and low-income students' rates of graduation: "About a quarter of college freshmen born into the bottom half of the income distribution will manage to collect a bachelor's degree by age 24, while almost 90 percent of freshmen born into families in the top income quartile will go on to finish their degree" (Tough). Further, even nonacademic experiences at college can be framed by social class. A 2013 Harvard University book by Armstrong and Hamilton, *Paying for the Party: How Colleges Maintains Inequality*, traced the ways that university and social structures facilitate upward class mobility for affluent students whose class background influenced their social groups, majors, and extracurricular activities, preserving what the authors call a "pathway to privilege," while low-income students lacked the benefits provided by college-educated and high-income parents. Jessica Valenti summarizes the intersection of class and gender, emphasizing from Armstrong and Hamilton's study that "Regardless of the success, class impacted almost every aspect of the college women's lives—even sexual assault. Female students who had parents who went to college were able to warn their daughters about the tactics of fraternity predators, and were actually less likely to be targeted because, as Armstrong and Hamilton write, 'insulting a highly ranked woman in a top sorority was akin to affronting her whole sorority.' Lower-income students—especially those women who were perceived as garish—were more likely to be assaulted and less likely to be believed" (Valenti, 'How to End").

Another important point is that working-class and poverty-class students who *do* manage to succeed are often pointed to as proof that structural inequality does not exist, which is not only a mistake but cruel when an individual's success is used to berate those who, because of structural inequality, are unable to follow suit. Neither is our point to diminish or dismiss the success that middle- and upper-class students achieve through hard work; rather, the point is to acknowledge the enabling conditions that provided a context for those students' hard work in the first place.

One final point: the class-based structural barriers to educational achievement are buttressed by controlling images of working-class and poverty-class people as dumb and buffoonish. These images and characterizations appear both in the news media and in popular culture, from Homer Simpson to MTV's short-lived reality TV series "Buckwild." In other words, ideology purports to show that working-class and poverty-class people of all races and ethnicities are poor as a result of both poor choices and lesser innate intelligence.

As the previous illustrations suggest, the bootstraps myth serves an important function in suggesting that certain kinds of privilege and oppression (namely, economic) are irrelevant to social and educational achievement even though there is strong statistical and demographic data to suggest that those social indicators have a great deal of power over who achieves traditional markers of success in the United States.

Internalized Oppression and Horizontal Hostility

Institutional and ideological manifestations of privilege and oppression are internalized by members of both dominant and marginalized groups. In other words, it is often the case that members of marginalized groups come to internalize the dominant group's characterizations of them as lesser and inferior. This phenomenon is called **internalized oppression**, and can be seen as a marker of the "success" of the dominant group's use of ideology. For example, when the working class and poor people internalize classism, they come to believe that their class position is deserved, that their failure to succeed economically is the result of their failure to work hard enough and exert enough effort to achieve class mobility. Gay men and lesbians internalize heterosexism if they accept the belief that they are unfit to parent or are undeserving of protection from discrimination. Women internalize sexism if they come to believe that they are less capable in mathematics and the natural sciences.

A related concept is that of *horizontal hostility*, whereby members of marginalized groups police each other's behavior and/or appearance. Horizontal hostility happens when a member of a marginalized group identifies with the values of the dominant group. The phenomenon of women slut shaming other women is an example of horizontal hostility. Armstrong and Hamilton's book is useful again here. As reported on the online magazine *Slate*, the research found that "'high status' and 'low-status,' or class-based perceptions differed, with the low-status women pinning sluttiness on 'rich bitches in sororities,' and the high-status women aligning sluttiness with women they perceived as 'trashy,' not 'classy.' This class-based construction of the campus slut allowed both groups to deflect the stigma of 'sluttiness' onto other women and away from themselves, establish hierarchies among social groups, and police everyone's gender performance—including their own—along the way" (Hess). In this way, college women participated in a gender system that they themselves propped up as a way of both surveilling others' sexual conduct and justifying their own.

Systems of oppression and privilege are internalized by individuals, then, and as such, these systems have a psychological dimension that must be addressed when working to dismantle them. As Audre Lorde writes, "For we have, built into all of us, old blueprints of expectation and response, old structures of oppression, and these must be altered at the same time as we alter the living conditions which are a result of those structures" (123).

Anchoring Topics through the Lens of Privilege and Oppression
Work and Family

Two institutions that profoundly shape women's lives are the workplace and the family; both have elements of formal and informal institutions. For example, workplaces are governed and authorized by a variety of laws, acts, and policies regarding labor, safety, and leave for illness or family obligations. Additionally, although family structure is not subject necessarily to particular laws, acts, or policies, particular family structures may be reinforced, acknowledged, or ignored by those policies and laws. Such institutional structures manifest privilege and oppression in several key ways, including incentivizing marriage and, conversely, limiting social support for gender-equitable policies that would promote female self-sufficiency.

U.S. social policy reflects the dominant ideology idealizing the nuclear family in several key ways that conflict with the reality of the family lives of most U.S. women. For example, looking at the statistical and demographic realities of women, marriage, and motherhood reveals how misaligned the relationship between family structures and responsibilities is with workplace and public policies, structures that subsequently oppress women—poor women and women of color most of all. Of all mothers with children under the age of 18, 70.6% participated in the labor force, according to the Bureau of Labor Statistics numbers from 2010 and 2011. The participation rate for married mothers with a spouse present was slightly lower (68.7%) than those who were single, divorced, or separated (74.6%). Further, although women were less likely to be in the labor force when their children were not of school age, a majority of women with children under the age of 6 participated in the labor force (63.9%), and even a majority of women with infants less than 1 year old worked outside the home (55.8%). The majority of women with children work outside the home, and as the *New York Times* reported recently, 51% of women in 2005 reported living without a spouse, up from 35% in 1950 and 49% in 2000, noting that married couples are now a minority of all American households (Swarns). This shift has been attributed to a number of factors, including later ages for first marriage and cohabitation for longer periods before marriage. In addition, while divorce rates have stabilized overall, a growing number of people are choosing not to marry, or not to remarry after getting divorced or being widowed. There is a particularly striking change evident among middle-aged Americans. Reporting on a recent study that appeared in *The Gerontologist*, Rachel Swarns notes that "About a third of adults ages 46 through 64 were divorced, separated or had never been married in 2010, compared with 13 percent in 1970."

It is also necessary to add race as a variable when looking at marriage statistics; according to U.S. Census figures, only about 30% of black women are living with a spouse, compared with 49% of Hispanic women, 55% of non-Hispanic white women, and more than 60% of Asian women. Marriage rates also differ dramatically by class. Many statistics use education level as a proxy for class, and it is certainly the case that there is a strong connection between the two. According to June Carbone and Naomi Cahn, "Today, the likelihood of marrying, staying married, and raising children within marriage correlates strongly with education. Indeed, for white college graduates the non-marital birth rate has stayed at 2%; for African American high school dropouts, it's 96%. In between is a steeply slanted line that links family form to education, income, and race."

Our societal institutions and many of our governmental policies have not kept pace with these changes, but this failure of alignment means that some women can expect to navigate systems with privilege whereas others will find themselves experiencing oppression by those same institutions. In some cases this gap or mismatch can be characterized in terms of a time lag; that is, we can expect that our institutions and policies haven't caught up with the pace of change (but they eventually will), but in other instances the gap or mismatch represents deliberate efforts to stem the tide of changes to family structure based on the belief that these changes are problematic and even destructive. This has taken the form of incentivizing particular behaviors such as marriage or eliminating social support programs that unmarried mothers use to support themselves and their children. Two relevant policies are the **Family and**

Medical Leave Act of 1993 (FMLA) and the Personal Responsibility and Work Opportunity Reconciliation Act of 1996. An analysis of these policies show how these realities of family structure and labor force participation by women are misaligned with current public policies that support work–life balance, that allow women to fully participate in the workplace, and that promote particular sorts of female economic dependence while discouraging and stigmatizing others, resulting in privilege for some women and oppression for others.

The FMLA illustrates how public policy has not kept pace with changes in women's roles and women's workforce participation—and the resistance to establishing the policy shows how ideologies can determine material realities. Pregnancy, lactation, and child care are a regular part of many women's life course, but it wasn't until 1993 under President Clinton that the United States adopted the FMLA, the first step toward ensuring that women could retain the right to return to their jobs after any leave to accommodate family needs. Although the passage of the FMLA represented a positive first step toward creating policy that would help make workplaces more accommodating of the needs of women workers, this Act has several limitations. First, FMLA provides a good example of how it privileges certain women but does not serve others: workers may only avail themselves of its benefits if they have worked a certain number of hours within a year and if they work for an employer with more than 50 employees. The Act may not protect their right to return to their exact position, only a similar one within that workplace. For professional women who work full time and who have access to a second wage in their household, FMLA may cover their needs. However, FMLA provides only unpaid leave, and unless a specific workplace complements this leave with paid leave, most women who are not partnered with a second wage earner may not be able to take the full 12 weeks of unpaid leave.

In these regards, the current legislative protection for women lags far behind that of other countries. As the Project on Global Working Families has documented in its report, *The Work, Family, and Equity Index*, of 173 countries studied, 168 offer guaranteed leave with some associated income in connection with childbirth; 98 countries offer 14 weeks or more of paid leave. The United States offers none (see Figure 3.3).

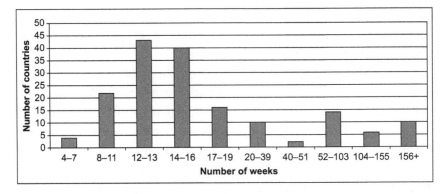

Figure 3.3 Maximum Paid Leave (Maternity & Parental) Available to Mothers in Countries Providing Paid Leave

Further, despite overwhelming scientific evidence in support of mothers' breastfeeding of infants, the United States only minimally supports and protects breastfeeding mothers legislatively. As the Centers for Disease Control reports, mothers are the "fastest-growing segment of the U.S. Labor Force." With the passage of the 2010 Affordable Healthcare Act, employers are now required to "provide reasonable break time and a private, non-bathroom place for nursing mothers to express breast milk during the workday, for one year after the child's birth" (United States Breastfeeding Committee). Although this is a welcome policy, not all workplaces are covered under the law (the law contains an exemption for workplaces with fewer than 50 employees), and there is a long way to go in terms of raising awareness and ensuring compliance.

Additionally, although some states have legislation protecting women's right to breastfeed in public, three have no such legislation, and just 12 have a protective law with an enforcement provision.[1] As we discuss in Chapter 4, breastfeeding support and resources are also particularly tied to social class and the types of work environments that are amenable to promoting a climate friendly for lactating mothers. Women working in salaried, professional positions are more likely to have access to unmonitored breaks and private working spaces that will allow them to pump or breastfeed. What this means is that these laws and policies offer protection to women with class privilege, often in stable work environments with greater levels of autonomy, whereas other women will be disempowered by their workplaces.

Despite these demographic realities, public policies have routinely reproduced ideologies that are at odds with women's lived realities and that privilege particular kinds of family structures and social statuses while marginalizing others. Other types of governmental protections for life events that are particular to women illustrate how privilege and oppression operate structurally to promote particular types of conduct and choices for women and reduce other, socially stigmatized and regressive choices. The lack of access to paid family leave presupposes acceptable forms of dependence for women—specifically, dependence on a second (usually male) wage earner to support her reproductive activities. Further, reforms to Aid to Families with Dependent Children (colloquially known as "welfare") and accompanying programs become a form of structural oppression for poor women and, often, women of color.

Social Construction of Motherhood

The 1996 Personal Responsibility and Work Opportunity Reconciliation Act (PRWORA) replaced Aid to Families with Dependent Children (which provided cash benefits to recipients) with the new program Temporary Assistance for Needy Families (TANF). Generally referred to as "welfare reform," the Act made some significant revisions to support benefits available to recipients, including placing a lifetime limit of 60 months on recipients, mandating work outside the home or work-seeking behaviors, and more stringent consequences for failure to comply with the program requirements. The social construction of motherhood as reflected in public policy illustrates ideologies about the "mythical norm" described previously, as well as heterosexism, racism, and classism.

The ideological assumptions underpinning welfare reform reflect the threshold concept of privilege and oppression around gender, class, and race. For example, the policy changes reinforce the notion that particular forms of dependence—dependence on a male breadwinner—are acceptable forms (and the nuclear family is an ideal to which all families with children should aspire) while reflecting a prevailing assumption that financial dependence on government benefits should be curbed. In other words, women with children born out of wedlock cannot expect to support themselves with government assistance because of the idealization of male breadwinning. This is illustrated by the inclusion of "Marriage Promotion" policies and funding embedded in the PRWORA—a set of policies and allocated resources dedicated toward promoting marriage, particularly out of concern from social conservatives that providing financial support to poor women created a disincentive to marry. Provisions of the bill supported public advertising campaigns on the value of marriage, the support of high school curricula promoting marriage, premarital education and training, marriage workshops, and divorce reduction programs focused on relationship skills (Dailard). The privileging of the heteronormative family—and the consequent structural oppression that results from the imposition of one ideological perspective on family configuration, particularly on poor women—present clear evidence that race, class, and gender are central in determining social location and status.

Assumptions that undergird the welfare reform efforts of the mid 1990s do not account for the individual circumstances and social location of those who avail themselves of government assistance. For example many TANF recipients face significant barriers to employment. As the Office of Public Affairs notes, 42% of welfare recipients did not have a high school diploma or its equivalent; another one-third had serious health issues; and about one-third did not have recent work experience that would make them employable. Recipients often faced additional challenges to paid employment including young infants at home, language barriers, or care responsibilities for family members/ children with disabilities. Policies aimed at marriage promotion discount the personal autonomy of women with multiple responsibilities by channeling resources into the promotion of an ideological ideal that is based on male dominance and **compulsory heterosexuality**. As Marcella Gemelli observes in her 2008 study of low-income mothers, much of welfare reform was politically motivated around the value of "independence and self-sufficiency," which is, as Gemelli notes, "advocating for independence and self-sufficiency through working for wages, yet encouraging marriage seems contradictory" (102). Certainly the subtext of such policy efforts is that certain kinds of dependence are more acceptable than others, particularly those that support patriarchal values.

Critics have also examined the representations of certain acceptable types of motherhood, including young and teenage motherhood. Public discourse swirled around the launching of the MTV shows "16 and Pregnant" and "Teen Mom," which detailed the decision-making and lives of teenage girls experiencing unintended pregnancies. However, as *Time* magazine pointed out, "In 2005, African-American women from the ages of 15-to-19 became pregnant at three times the rate of white women in America. But *Teen Mom*'s four main cast members are all white, as are the majority of subjects on *16 and Pregnant*" (Sun). Filmic representations such as the 2007 film *Juno* focus on young, white teenage girls navigating unintended pregnancies, drawing attention to the issue, but present a narrow and demographically distorted image of the realities of teenage pregnancy in the United States, illustrating how ideologies are circulated through media in ways that may privilege some groups and oppress or even erase others.

On the flip side of incentivizing marriage for low-income heterosexuals is the history of restricting marriage both among members of marginalized groups, and between members of marginalized groups and dominant groups. As an example of the latter, until the Supreme Court's landmark decision in **Loving v. Virginia** in 1967 declared such miscegenation laws unconstitutional, many states still prohibited interracial marriage. Today's most pressing example of laws restricting marriage is same-sex marriage. The number of states that authorize same-sex marriage is on the increase, with the pace quickening considerably after the Supreme Court declared Section 3 of the **Defense of Marriage Act (DOMA)** unconstitutional in the early summer of 2013. The federal government now recognizes same-sex marriages regardless of whether the state in which the couple resides recognizes the marriage.

When DOMA was passed in 1996, it was barely debated and was passed by a huge margin in both the Senate and the House. Less than two decades later, it would appear that the tide is turning with regard to marriage equality, with polls taken in the spring of 2013 consistently showing that over 50% of Americans support it. This growing acceptance is certainly a result of generational change, with polls reporting that between 70 and 80% of Americans under the age of 30 support marriage equality. The shift is not solely driven by young people, however; a significant number of people in older demographics report that their opinion on same-sex marriage has changed, often as a result of knowing someone who is a member of the LGBTQ community.

Contrasting how marriage is incentivized for some and prohibited for others illustrates how oppression and privilege operate through government as a societal institution. The right to marry is an example of heterosexual privilege, although this is a dynamic process that is in the process of change. It is important to remember, however, that marriage, as a heterosexual institution, was historically a site of oppression for women. Assuming that same-sex marriage is legalized in the coming decade, it will be important to study and track whether and to what extent same-sex couples transform the institution, as opposed to being transformed by it.

Language, Images, and Symbols

Privilege and oppression manifest in symbolic ways as well as material ways (for example, language and images versus material conditions such as institutions like work and education). Three key examples illustrate privilege and oppression:

"Mansplaining"

In 2008, author Rebecca Solnit published the piece "Men Explain Things to Me," a more cerebral and socially conscious meditation on the neologism subsequently coined **mansplaining**, or as urbandictionary. com has defined it, "To explain in a patronizing manner, assuming total ignorance on the part of those listening. The mansplainer is often shocked and hurt when their mansplanation is not taken as absolute fact, criticized or even rejected altogether." Subsequently, the "mansplanation" phenomenon has circulated over social media including Facebook pages, blogs, and Tumblr sites that document the experience of privilege and oppression that Solnit experienced. In her short essay, Solnit originally described a dinner party experience where a male guest insisted on describing a new book he had read about, summarizing its thesis and holding forth on the topic until realizing, only after several interruptions by another party guest, that Solnit herself was the author of the book under discussion. What Solnit ultimately tries to show is that, although for some women mansplaining may be a minor "social misery", for others she argues, "At the heart of the struggle of feminism to give rape, date rape, marital rape, domestic violence, and workplace sexual harassment legal standing as crimes has been the necessity of making women credible and audible." Solnit takes up the question of privilege and oppression by asserting "This goes way beyond Men Explaining Things, but it's part of the same archipelago of arrogance." That is, mansplaining raises the question of *who has the authority* to speak and who is credible when speaking. The phenomenon of women's online contributions similarly engages the topic of privilege and oppression.

Online Presence and Wikipedia

As the increasingly ubiquitous source of information for online users, Wikipedia is an important part of the construction of knowledge and popular access to knowledge on the widest range of topics of practically any compendium, print or online. A number of new studies (and subsequent activist work) have centered on the gender disparity in the type and quality of contributions and edits made to Wikipedia, as well as the virtual environment experienced by Wikipedia contributors.

Research published by the Association of Computing Machinery and cosponsored by Yahoo showed that women editors of Wikipedia made fewer revisions in numbers to entries but made qualitatively more robust and fuller revisions, even though they make up an overall total of just 18% of Wikipedia editors. Other research estimates female contributions at 9–15% of editors. Research from the University of Minnesota's GroupLens Research Lab offered three key findings in their 2011 examination of over 110,000 Wikipedia editors: in terms of sheer numbers, just 16% of editors identified as women. They observed that women editors were more likely than men to leave or cease editing, particularly when, as newcomers, their edits were challenged or "reverted." In 2014, the Isla Vista, California, shooting tragedy became the subject of a social media and Wikipedia battle illustrating this online tension. Shooter Elliot Rodger killed six people and investigations revealed his self-reported motivation to fulfill what he himself called his "war on women" (Covarrubias). Harnessing the power of social media in response to the tragedy, women took to **Twitter** with the hashtag **#yesallwomen** to call out violence and sexism; this hashtag served as a counterpoint and challenge to the previously existing tag, **#notallmen**, which was created by men's rights activists to contradict the effort to make visible and to critique sexism and violence. A battle for control over the message around the shooting became visible in the Wikipedia page (an information source for many readers and Internet users) over how the shooting and subsequent social media coverage was presented. One draft of the entry specifically identified Rodger's misogyny as his motivation for the shooter, while a counteredit charged that such claims reflected "feminist propaganda" and "misandry" (Dries). The Wikipedia entries for "#YesAllWomen" and "Isla Vista Shootings" saw heated disagreement on the discussion page about how this tragic event could be discussed in terms that critique male privilege and made visible women's oppression.

A second area of investigation concluded that topics traditionally of greater interest to women received less attention than those that have been historically of interest to men. For example, discussions of films aimed at female audiences were shorter or of lower quality than those with primarily male audiences, leading researchers to conclude "Wikipedia seems to be growing in a way that is biased toward topics of interest to males."

Finally, in terms of the community and culture of Wikipedia editing, the researchers observed, in conflicts among editors, entries by women were more likely to be "undone" than those of men, and female editors were more likely than male editors to be "indefinitely blocked." Sue Gardner, Executive Director of the Wikimedia Foundation, explains in her blog that women's contributions to Wikipedia are inhibited or discouraged for a variety of reasons, ranging from hostile editing tactics (for example, editing wars over the difference between identifying a rape scene in a film as a "sex scene" and meeting the standards of "neutrality"), to the unfriendly interface, to men's greater level of self-confidence and willingness to speak with authority, to the conflict-heavy culture. The

"Gender Gap Manifesto" appears on the Wikimedia foundation and aims to "foster an environment where people can express their thoughts, feelings, and solutions regarding the gender gap on Wikipedia. The goal is to collaboratively find solutions to improve the presence of women on Wikipedia and its sister projects." Collective action online—in the form of **crowdsourcing**—is one way that women from a variety of positions are aiming to change the culture of online contributions to Wikipedia to make it a more welcoming space for women to contribute and to challenge an online culture that is exclusionary, adversarial, or belittling. In this way, privilege and oppression are demonstrated by the ways that women's voices are more systematically closed off whereas men's voices are dominant.

Marked vs. Unmarked in Language

In the early days of second-wave feminism, much attention was paid to the ways in which sexism was embedded in language. This feminist critique of language took many forms, including a critique of the default use of masculine pronouns in English and the default use of masculine-gendered occupational titles like "mailman," "fireman," "chairman," and "congressman." While these critiques resulted in widespread change, it is also clear that there are significant ways in which oppression and privilege continue to play out in language.

One of the markers of privilege is invisibility, and one of the ways this invisibility manifests is through identity terms and labels. In other words, dominant groups that are a part of the mythical norm have the privilege of being unmarked and unremarkable because of their presumed neutrality and normality. To return to the term transgender that was introduced in Chapter 2, for example, current usage of the term refers to people whose gender identity is at odds with their birth-assigned gender, but until very recently there was no term to describe people whose gender identity is consistent with their birth-assigned gender. The term *cisgender* was coined to fill this vacuum, and arguably to draw attention to, and make visible, the privilege of the dominant group. In *Transgender History*, Susan Stryker explains that the term cisgendered "names the usually unstated assumption of nontransgender status contained in the words 'man' and 'woman'" (22). Another example comes from politicized groups within the autism community; they have coined the term *neurotypical* to describe people who are not on the autism spectrum. To be in the unmarked group is to be considered the default norm.

A slight variation on this point comes from considering when we do and don't attach qualifiers to our descriptions of and references to people and institutions; for example, it is still fairly common practice to specify race only when referring to a person of color, to specify gender when referring to women, to specify sexual identity when referring to someone who is gay, lesbian, or bisexual, and so forth. As Michael Kimmel wryly points out, "A white person will be happy to tell you about a 'black friend,' but when that same person simply mentions a 'friend,' everyone will assume the person is white" (3). Similarly, marriage is frequently modified with the word "gay" when referring to same-sex couples. As GLAAD's "Ally's Guide to Terminology" points out, however, "Just as it would be inappropriate to call the marriage of two older adults "elder marriage," it is inappropriate to call the marriage of a same-sex couple 'gay marriage' or 'same-sex marriage.' Simply talk about *marriage* instead." The argument here is that marriage is marriage regardless of the sex of the couple.

Another example returns us to Wikipedia and a controversy over categories. An editor broke up the category of "American Novelists" by removing most of the women and listing them separately and exclusively as "American Women Novelists." The category of American novelists, then, was becoming a list almost exclusively of male writers, although it was not named as such. As in the other examples, the default assumption is that the category of American novelists is implicitly coded male and masculine. Rock music also tends to be coded as male and masculine, such that reviews of the work of women musicians and assessments of their status as a group in rock lump them all together and judge them in relation to the work of male musicians. Artist Neko Case made headlines in 2014 when she lost her temper on Twitter after a journalist in *Playboy* reviewed her latest album somewhat reductively in terms of gender; she and other women have grown tired of seeing their work

Figure 3.4 Jane George

understood solely or primarily as the work of a woman first and a musician second.

Contributors to the blog Sociological Images have documented this phenomenon of **marked and unmarked** language as it plays out in public signage, as well as in product packaging and products themselves; new examples of this phenomenon continue to be added to the Pinterest site as they are discovered. For example, one posted photo shows an end-of-aisle sign in the health and beauty section of a big-box store that describes what customers will find in that aisle; it lists "Deodorant" and "Women's Deodorant." Figure 3.4 shows an example of this phenomenon in children's toy packaging. In the examples they document, maleness is an unmarked, invisible category, and only girls/women have a gender.

This illustrates how the mythical norm and unearned privilege manifest in language, although the example about the coinage of new terms to name dominant groups that are a part of the mythical norm shows that language can also be harnessed to bring previously invisible privilege to light.

Women's Bodies

Privilege and oppression are illustrated in several aspects of the way that patriarchal culture attempts to exert control over women's reproductive choices and their sexuality.

For example, the patriarchal birthing industry in the United States reveals how privilege and oppression function in terms of controlling women's bodies. Within the medical industry, the four values of patriarchal culture identified by Allan Johnson (a society that is male dominated, male identified, male centered, and obsessed with control) are evident and reveal women's oppression within the infrastructure, policy, and practices that reframe childbirth from a natural part of a woman's reproductive life cycle to a medical event of a pathological nature often requiring pharmaceutical and sometimes even surgical intervention.

As the report "Evidence-Based Maternity Care" illustrates, many interventions to physiological childbirth are overused, while those that can offer equal benefit are underused, with women's ability to achieve physiological childbirth often undermined or questioned through medical practices. As the report explains, "many practices that are disproved or appropriate for mothers and babies only in limited circumstances are in wide use. Conversely, numerous beneficial practices are underused because they offer limited scope for economic gain, are less compatible with predominant medical values and practices, or have only recently been favorably evaluated" (9). In a culture that privileges control, efficiency, and convenience over tolerance for the timing uncertainties of natural processes such as labor and delivery, the overuse of convenience methods such as induction of labor, episiotomies, and vacuum- and forceps-assisted deliveries predominate at levels well beyond the logical benefits to women and babies:

Table 3.2

Intervention or Practice	2000–2002	2005	2011–2012
Care provider used drugs or some other technique to try to cause labor to begin	44%	41%	41%
Had epidural or spinal analgesia for pain relief	63%	76%	67%
Midwife attended baby's birth	10%	8%	10%
Had narcotics intravenously for pain relief	30%	22%	16%
Used no pain medication	20%	14%	17%
Doula provided supportive care during birth	5%	3%	6%
Obstetrician/gynecologist attended birth	80%	79%	70%
Family physician attended birth	4%	7%	6%
Had a spontaneous vaginal birth	64%	61%	59%
Had forceps or vacuum extraction	11%	7%	11%
Had cesarean section	24%	32%	31%
Used immersion in tub or pool for comfort	na	6%	8%
Used shower for comfort	na	4%	10%
Drank anything during labor	35%	43%	41%
Ate anything during labor	14%	15%	20%
Gave birth lying on back	na	57%	68%
Episiotomy	35%	25%	17%
Women who indicated a desire to exclusively breastfeed who received formula or water to supplement breast milk	47%	38%	29%

Data provided by the *Listening to Mothers Surveys*[2] conducted by Childbirth Connection

A good example of this kind of intervention beyond levels of sound medical practice is the increase in deliveries by cesarean section. The rate of cesarean section—or surgical intervention in childbirth, both emergency and planned—has skyrocketed in the last several decades. As Sakala and Corry document, the C-section rate in the United States rose from 9.5% as recently as 1990 to 22.3% in 2005, and in 2010, the rate had risen to 32.8%, nearly a third of all births (Centers for Disease Control). The World Health Organization (WHO) estimated in 2010 that, in 2008, some 6.2 million C-sections were performed unnecessarily (and another 3.18 million should have been performed, primarily in developing countries with little access to advanced medical technology and facilities). In 1985, WHO declared, "There is no justification for any region to have C-section rates higher than 10–15%" (Gibbons 4). In terms of privilege and oppression, these data reveal how the patriarchal medical profession imposes assumptions and values that serve to control women's choices, to naturalize the medicalization of childbirth, and to present differential (and often medically inferior) care to a specific group served by this institution (women).

Globally, the issue of female genital cutting—sometimes called female circumcision—is a particularly clear example of how women's sexuality is controlled for particular cultural purposes attached to women's low status. As WHO explains, "Female genital mutilation (FGM) includes procedures that intentionally alter or cause injury to the female genital organs for non-medical reasons" and can range from the removal of the clitoris to excising the clitoris and parts of the labia minora to full infibulation, which narrows the vaginal opening and sometimes also includes a clitoridectomy. Female genital cutting is performed on young girls, usually before the age of 15, and the purpose is rooted in deep cultural notions of women's sexual purity and marriageability. Its intention is to reduce or eliminate women's enjoyment of sexual intercourse and to prevent women from engaging in sexual activity, as a way to ensure chastity. In many cultures where the procedure is performed, women's social and cultural values are attached primarily to their marital status, and cutting is intended to assure women's virginity and fidelity which ultimately communicates their marriageability. Over 140 million girls and women have experienced female circumcision, with 100 million of them located in Africa. Ultimately, female circumcision is a product of women's low and limited cultural status and illustrates, according to many feminist critics, the ways that girls and women are oppressed because of this practice that ties their identities to their marriageability and limits their ability to experience sexual pleasure.

A final example of privilege and oppression related to women's bodies is what we referred to as "rape culture" in Chapter 2, or the idea that sexual violence is socially tolerated and woven into the fabric of society through various forms of sexism, victim blaming, support for male dominance and female passivity, and legal and policy structures that place responsibility for male sexuality on women. This is part of control and oppression because the burden for preventing sexual violence is carried primarily by women who are expected to limit their behavior, actions, dress, and other aspects of their daily life to minimize the likelihood that they will be victimized. An alternative model would place the primary responsibility on all men to engage in conduct that creates safe communities, workplaces, and homes for the women in their lives. In this regard, women's oppression is illustrated by the mental self-monitoring that many must continually do to assess themselves, their surroundings, and their conduct for threats of violence or "gender-based miscommunications," whereas men's privilege is illustrated by the fact that they are typically not expected to monitor themselves or their conduct for safety and security and freedom from sexual violence.

Learning Roadblock

"If I don't see it, it must not exist." One of the biggest barriers many students experience in understanding the "big picture" or structural contexts of privilege and oppression is the temptation to use one's own experience as a "measuring stick." For example, it may be hard to grasp the enormity of rates of violence against women if it is an issue that has not touched one's life personally. Julie Zeilinger calls this the "If I don't see it, it must not exist" mentality, and she argues that this mentality is often a product of being unaware of our privileges. The important point to remember here is that although personal experience is a critical source of knowledge in Women's and Gender Studies, it also has to be measured against other kinds of knowledge that can provide a framework within which to place one's personal experience, and to compare it with the experiences of others. Students who are learning to think, know, and see like Women's and Gender Studies practitioners learn to position their own experiences and awareness of the world alongside the statistical, demographic, and theoretical knowledge gained by systematic evidence collection by researchers, as well as the varying perspectives that their classmates and conversation partners can bring to their understanding. What this means is that new students of Women's and Gender Studies should think about how their own personal experience is reflective of others' gendered experiences of the world, and how it departs from others' experiences.

Case Study

Renewal of the Violence against Women Act (2012): In 2012, the Violence Against Women Act (VAWA), a comprehensive piece of legislation with multiple provisions, was up for reauthorization. The initial Act, passed in 1994, focused on a multipronged approach to intervening in and preventing violence against women, including criminal justice responsiveness and improving services to victims. Three provisions in the 2012 reauthorization illustrate structural forms of oppression that reveal the oppression of particular groups, the privilege of other groups, and the role of institutions and ideology in shaping access to power and resources.

Since its adoption in 1994, VAWA has had a significant impact on incidents of violence; according to the White House, a 60% decline in incidents of violence against women can be attributed to the passage of the Act. In 2012, the reauthorization of the Act was held up by objections to several provisions designed to close loopholes and address gaps in the Act's coverage.

Rates of violence against Native women are significantly higher than for the overall rates of violence against women, with about a third encountering assaults and 60% experiencing intimate partner violence; they are also 2.5 times as likely to be raped as the overall rate of rape in the United States. However, combating such incidents is complicated by the fact that tribal law enforcement and courts only have jurisdiction over Native offenders against crimes committed on tribal land; as the White House reports, "tribes cannot prosecute a non-Indian, even if he lives on the reservation and is married to a tribal member." As a result, nonnative abusers are only subject to prosecution by federal law enforcement—who *do* have jurisdiction but who are often significantly far from the reservation and may be overburdened by other responsibilities, which results in sluggish and apathetic responses (Weisman). In discussions about the Act's reauthorization, the proposed solution to this gap was to allow Native American police and courts to pursue and prosecute non-Indians who commit acts of violence on tribal land; however, opponents argued that this provision would deny defendants their constitutional rights and rejected this compromise, leaving women who are already among the most vulnerable with no legal or policy recourse to addressing these crimes.

Objections were also offered on the basis of the expansion of services to LGBTQ victims and to undocumented immigrants. Despite national research showing that 45% of LGBTQ victims were refused services when they sought help at shelters, the bill stalled over political debates about whether services should be extended to cover victims in same-sex relationships. Further, although undocumented immigrants who had been victims of intimate partner violence could previously gain access to visas that would provide them "amnesty" in the United States, the proposed update to VAWA would expand the number of such visas available (Deruy). Ultimately, the legislation passed with the support of President Obama and both houses of Congress, in February 2013.

End of Chapter Elements

Evaluating Prior Knowledge

- Write briefly about how and in what context you have heard the term "privilege" before. Generate at least five examples of how this language is commonly used. Then discuss how your understanding has changed after reading Chapter 3.

Application Exercise

- Consider the opening illustration about Kathrine Switzer's entry in the Boston Marathon in 1967. In conversation with a partner or in an informal writing activity, think about how the key concepts from this chapter are illustrated by Switzer's story:
  - privilege
  - oppression
  - institutions
  - ideologies

Skills Assessment/Check for Understanding

- Consider the following scenarios. How are each examples of institutionalized oppression?
  - *redlining* (the practice of denying, or making inaccessible certain services such as insurance, home lending, and/or employment opportunities in order to control the racial or ethnic makeup of a geographical area). Visit the Fair Housing Center's website on Housing Segregation in Boston[3] for a historical overview and case study of a particular region.

- *segregated schools*: Visit the Library of Congress website "Brown vs. Board at Fifty:[4] "With an Even Hand, A Century of Racial Segregation, 1849–1950" for an overview of segregated schooling.
- *The Family and Medical Leave Act (1993)*: the policy implementation that allows for up to 12 weeks of unpaid leave for the birth or adoption of a child, illness, or to care for a family member. Visit the Office of Personnel Management's website, "Fact Sheet: Family and Medical Leave"[5] for an overview of the policy.
- *voucher programs*: the practice of using government funding to reimburse families for enrolling their children in private schools. See the National Conference of State Legislature's website, "School Vouchers"[6] for an overview.
- *hospital visitation policies*: the rights for same-sex couples to visit partners during hospitalization. Read the "Healthcare Equality Index: Equal Visitation"[7] page on the Human Rights Campaign's website for an overview.

Discussion Questions and Classroom Activities

1. Review the Case Study on violence in Native communities. In what ways does the case study illustrate the threshold concepts of privilege and oppression?
2. Select a term or concept from the chapter that seems "muddy" to you. With a partner, talk through the muddiness. What is creating a learning block? Why is it difficult? What would clarify it for you? Use a strategy called a "difficulty log" to map out the parts of the idea that are challenging you, including background knowledge you wish you had, challenging or confusing vocabulary, unclear relationships to other chapter concepts or other chapters, or unfamiliarity to your experience.
3. *Related activity*: Once you've had a chance to work through a muddy/difficult concept, try your hand at writing a "Misconception Alert" or "Learning Roadblock" like those featured in the chapter in order to spell out (a) what the learning challenge is and (b) how other students can overcome it.

Writing Prompts

1. Choose one of the issues from the Skills Assessment/Check for Understanding (redlining, school segregation, family and medical leave, voucher programs, hospital visitation) and write a formal essay in which you identify how public policy and cultural assumptions operate to support or dismantle oppressive structures and practices.
2. Read this column by Tim Wise on white privilege and the April 2013 Boston Marathon bombing: www.war-times.org/node/562. Using Wise's essay as a model, identify an example of some other kind of privilege—male privilege, heterosexual privilege, privilege based on ability—and write a similar critique.
3. Investigate a public policy that is in the news. How does the policy support equity or promote privilege and oppression for some groups over others?

Notes

1   www.ncsl.org/research/health/breastfeeding-state-laws.aspx#State
2   http://transform.childbirthconnection.org/wp-content/uploads/2013/06/LTM-III_Pregnancy-and-Birth.pdf
3   www.bostonfairhousing.org/timeline/1920s1948-Restrictive-Covenants.html
4   www.loc.gov/exhibits/brown/brown-segregation.html
5   www.opm.gov/policy-data-oversight/pay-leave/leave-administration/fact-sheets/family-and-medical-leave/
6   www.ncsl.org/research/education/school-choice-vouchers.aspx
7   www.hrc.org/resources/entry/healthcare-equality-index-equal-visitation

Works Cited and Suggested Readings

Antin, Judd, et al. "Gender Differences in Wikipedia Editing." *Wikisym.* October 2011. Web.

Armstrong, Elizabeth, and Laura Hamilton. Paying for the Party: How College Maintains Inequality. Cambridge, MA: Harvard UP, 2013. Print.

Bureau of Labor Statistics. "Economic News Release: Employment Characteristics of Families Summary." 26 April 2012. Web.

The Business of Being Born. Dir. Abby Epstein. New Line Home Entertainment, 2008. DVD.

Butler, Sarah Lorge. "How Kathrine Switzer Paved the Way." *ESPN.com.* 12 April 2012. Web.

Carbone, June, and Naomi Cahn. "Family Values? Conservative Economics Have Shredded Marriage Rates." *Next New Deal: The Blog of the Roosevelt Institute.* 9 August 2011. Web.

——. *Marriage Markets: How Inequality Is Remaking the American Family.* New York: Oxford UP, 2014. Print.

Centers for Disease Control and Prevention. "Births: Method of Delivery." 13 January 2013. Web.

Collins, Patricia Hill. *Black Feminist Thought: Knowledge, Consciousness, and the Politics of Empowerment.* New York: Routledge, 1991. Print.

Covarrubias, Amanda, Kate Mather, and Matt Stevens. "Isla Vista Shooting Suspect Targeted Sorority, Neighbors, Strangers." *Los Angeles Times.* 24 May 2014. Web.

Crittenden, Ann. *The Price of Motherhood: Why the Most Important Job in the World Is the Least Valued.* New York: Holt, 2002. Print.

Dailard, Cynthia. "Reproductive Health Advocates and Marriage Promotion: Asserting a Stake in the Debate." *The Guttmacher Report on Public Policy.* 8.1 (Feb 2005). Web.

Declerq, Eugene, et al. *Listening to Mothers, III: Report of the Third National U.S. Survey of Women's Childbearing Experiences.* Childcare Connection. May 2013. Web.

Department of Health and Human Services. "HHS Action Plan to Reduce Racial and Ethnic Health Disparities: A Nation Free of Disparities in Health and Health Care." Washington, DC, 2011. Web.

Deruy, Emily. "Senate Passes Domestic Violence Bill with New Key Protections." *ABC News.* 12 February 2013. Web.

Dries, Kate. "There's a Battle Going on over the Wikipedia Page for #YesAllWomen." *Jezebel.* 6 June 2014. Web.

Eagleton, Terry. *Literary Theory: An Introduction.* Minneapolis: U of Minnesota P, 1983. Print.

Edwards, Laurie. "The Gender Gap in Pain." *New York Times.* 16 March 2013. Web.

"Factsheet: The Violence against Women Act." *Whitehouse.gov.* 18 March 2013. Web.

"Family Income and Educational Attainment 1970–2009." *Postsecondary Education Opportunity: Public Policy Analysis of Opportunity for Postsecondary Education.* November 2010.

Ferber, Abby, and Michael Kimmel. *Privilege: A Reader.* 2nd ed. Boulder, CO: Westview P, 2010. Print.

Filipacchi, Amanda. "Wikipedia's Sexism Toward Female Novelists." *New York Times.* 24 April 2013. Web.

Frye, Marilyn. "Oppression." *The Feminist Philosophy Reader.* Ed. Alison Bailey and Chris Cuomo. New York: McGraw Hill, 2008. 41–49. Print.

Gardner, Sue. "Nine Reasons Women Don't Edit Wikipedia (In Their Own Words). *Sue Gardner's Blog.* 19 February 2011.

Gaskin, Ina May. *Spiritual Midwifery.* 4th ed. Summertown, TN: Book Publishing, 2002. Print.

Gemelli, Marcella. "Understanding the Complexity of Attitudes of Low-Income Single Mothers Toward Work and Family in the Age of Welfare Reform." *Gender Issues.* 25.101 (August 2008): 101–113. Web.

Gibbons, Luz, et al. "The Global Numbers and Costs of Additionally Needed and Unnecessary Caesarean Sections Performed per Year: Overuse as a Barrier to Universal Coverage." *World Health Report 2010. Background Paper (30).* 2010. Web.

Heldke, Lisa, and Peg O'Connor, eds. *Oppression, Privilege, and Resistance: Theoretical Perspectives on Racism, Sexism, and Heterosexism.* Boston: McGraw Hill, 2004. Print.

Hess, Amanda. "Are you a Slut? That Depends. Are you Rich?" *Slate.com.* 28 May 2014. Web.

Heymann, Jody, Alison Earle, and Jeffrey Hayes. *The Work, Family, and Equity Index: How Does the US Measure Up?* The Project on Global Working Families and the Institute for Health and Social Policy. No date. Web.

"How Class Works." Interactive Graphic. *New York Times.* 2005. Web.

Johnson, Allan. *Privilege, Power, and Difference.* Mountain View, CA: Mayfield, 2001. Print.

——. *The Gender Knot: Unraveling Our Patriarchal Legacy.* Philadelphia: Temple UP, 2005. Print.

Kimmel, Michael S. "Introduction: Toward a Pedagogy of the Oppressor." *Privilege: A Reader.* Michael S. Kimmel and Abby Ferber, eds. Boulder, CO: Westview, 1–10. Print.

Lears, T.J. Jackson. "The Concept of Cultural Hegemony: Problems and Possibilities." *American Historical Review.* 90.3 (June 1985): 567–593. Web.

Leistyna, Pepi. *Television and Working Class Identity: Intersecting Differences.* New York: Palgrave Macmillan, 2014. Print.

Lorde, Audre. "Age, Race, Class, and Sex: Women Redefining Difference." *Sister Outsider.* Trumansburg, NY: Crossing P, 1984.

Mantsios, Gregory. "Class in America—2006." *Race, Class, and Gender in the United States.* 7th ed. Ed. Paula Rothenberg. New York: Worth, 2007. 182–197. Print.

Matsuda, Mari. "Beside My Sister, Facing the Enemy: Legal Theory Out of Coalition." *Feminist Theory Reader: Local and Global Perspectives.* 3rd ed. Ed. Carole R. McCann and Seung-Kyung Kim. New York: Routledge, 2013. 332–342. Print.

Mcintosh, Peggy. "White Privilege: Unpacking the Invisible Knapsack." 1989. Web.

Mortensen, Tom. "Estimated Baccalaureate Degree Attainment by Age 24 by Family Income Quartile 1970 to 2012." *Postsecondary Education Opportunity.* November 2010. Web.

Pharr, Suzanne. *Homophobia: A Weapon of Sexism.* Berkeley, CA: Chardon P, 1997. Print.

Rooks, Noliwe. "*The Myth of Bootstrapping.*" *Time Magazine.* 7 September 2012. Web.

Sakala, Carol, and Maureen Corry. "Evidence-Based Maternity Care: What It Is and What It Can Achieve." Milbank Memorial Fund. 2008. Web.

Sandberg, Sheryl. "Why We Have Too Few Women Leaders." TEDTalks, December 2010. Web.

Solnit, Rebecca. "Men Explain Things to Me." *TomDispatch.com.* 13 April 2008. Web.

Starnes, Todd. "Public School Teaches 'White Privilege' Class." *Fox News.* 2013. Web.

Storey, John, ed. *Cultural Theory and Popular Culture: A Reader.* Harlow, England: Pearson/Prentice Hall. 3rd edition. 2006. Print.

Stryker, Susan. *Transgender History.* Seattle: Seal P, 2008. Print.

Sun, Feifei. "What MTV's *Teen Mom* Doesn't Deliver." *Time Magazine.* 14 July 2011. Web.

Swarns, Rachel. "More Americans Rejecting Marriage in 50s and Beyond." *New York Times.* 1 March 2012. Web.

Tatum, Beverly Daniel. "Defining Racism: Can We Talk?" *Women, Images and Realities: A Multicultural Anthology.* 3rd edition. Eds. Amy Kesselman, Lily McNair, and Nancy Schniedewind. Boston: McGraw-Hill, 2003. Print.

Tough, Paul. "Who Gets to Graduate?" *New York Times Magazine.* 15 May 2014. Web.

United States Breastfeeding Committee. "Existing Legislation." 2013. Web.

Urban Institute. "A Decade of Welfare Reform: Facts and Figures." *Office of Public Affairs.* June 2006. Web.

Valenti, Jessica. "How to End the College Class War." *Guardian.* 27 May 2014. Web.

Weisman, Jonathan. "Measure to Protect Women Stuck on Tribal Land Issue." *New York Times.* 10 February 2013. Web.

Wise, Tim. *White Like Me: Reflections on Race from a Privileged Son.* Brooklyn, NY: Skull P, 2005. Print.

World Health Organization. "Female Genital Mutilation." *World Health Organization Media Centre.* February 2013. Web.

Yamato, Gloria. "Something about the Subject Makes it Hard to Name." *Making Face, Making Soul.* Ed. Gloria Anzaldua. San Francisco: Aunt Lute Books, 1990. 25–30. Print.

Zeilinger, Julie. *A Little F'D Up: Why Feminism is Not a Dirty Word.* Berkeley, CA: Seal Press, 2012. Print.

Zurn, Rhonda. "University of Minnesota Researchers Reveal Wikipedia Gender Biases." 11 August 2011. Web.

Zwick, Rebecca. "Is the SAT a Wealth Test?" *Phi Delta Kappan.* 84.4 (December 2002): 307–311. Print.

4

INTERSECTIONALITY

Figure 4.1 Getty Images/AFP/THOMAS COEX

Opening Illustration

A good portion of the media coverage of the 2012 Summer Olympics, held in London, focused on the presence and performance of women athletes; indeed, some commentators referred to the 2012 Olympics as the "Women's Games" or the "Year of the Woman." The 2012 Olympics marked the first time that every participating country's team included women; women's overall participation represented an all-time high; and women represented over 40% of all participating athletes, a number that has risen significantly in the past two decades (women represented just 24% of athletes in the 1984 Summer Olympics held in Los Angeles). With the addition of women's boxing, the 2012 Olympics were the first in which women were included in every sport.

This is not to say, of course, that sexism has been magically eliminated from the Olympics and their coverage. Although women are now included in every sport, there are still more medaling opportunities for men. Female athletes are sexualized, and their bodies are often scrutinized and judged in relation to the beauty and body ideal (as opposed to an athletic ideal). A good example of this happened when media outlets suggested that Australian swimmer Leisel Jones was too heavy and not fit enough to compete in the Olympics. And women boxers narrowly avoided being required to wear skirts while competing; the Amateur International Boxing Association made skirts optional after many objections were made.

The Olympic Games, and sports more generally, is clearly an arena that is ripe for gender analysis. But whether we adopt a "glass half full" or "glass half empty" approach to our discussion, the analysis will be woefully short-sighted and one-dimensional unless we broaden our lens to consider gender in relation to race, class, sexual identity, and nation.

Consider, for example, the experience of Gabby Douglas, who won two gold medals in gymnastics in London, in the individual all-around and the team competitions. She was the first woman to win gold in both categories in the same Olympics. At first glance, then, her accomplishments fit easily within the "Year of the Woman" narrative. Alternately, we could maintain a single-axis lens but switch it to race; in doing that, we might focus on the fact that she was the first African American to win gold in the all-around competition. Her accomplishment of these "firsts" was a huge part of the media coverage about her during and after the Games. Those accomplishments threatened to be overshadowed, however, by discussion (which seems to have originated in social media and was then taken up by news media) about her hair. No, you didn't read that wrong; commenters scrutinized Douglas's hairstyle, calling her hair "unkempt." Understanding *why* her hair became the object of such scrutiny requires an intersectional approach. Put another way, if we try to analyze the comments and the subsequent media coverage solely as a gender issue, or solely as an issue of race, we would come up short, and have only a partial understanding of what was going on. An intersectional approach to this incident, by contrast, considers how both beauty standards and the sport of gymnastics are classed, gendered, and racialized, and also explores the class, gender, and racial identities of those who made the comments in the first place.

A feminist stance explores how systems of privilege and oppression intersect.

Why a Threshold Concept?

As previous chapters have asserted, in order to understand how individual social locations are shaped, it's important to see how systems of privilege and oppression intersect. This notion of "intersectionality" is at the heart of feminist analysis. As this chapter will explore, different groups benefit from or are disadvantaged by institutional structures, and this chapter will review how overlapping categories of identity profoundly shape our experiences within institutions. You should build on the learning you have done to this point about social constructionism and privilege and oppression in order to gain a greater understanding of those threshold concepts by applying an intersectional lens to your thinking. Although gender as a category of analysis is useful, it is incomplete without understanding that other categories of identity (race, sexuality, class, age, etc.) are equally as important in gaining accurate knowledge about people's lives and experiences. As Estelle Freedman asserts in *No Turning Back: The History of Feminism and the Future of Women*, "Feminists must continually criticize two kinds of false universals. We must always ask not only, 'What about women?' (what difference does gender make?) but also 'Which women?' (what difference do race, class, or nationality make?)" (8).

Definitions, Key Terms, and Illustrations

Intersectionality is a theoretical framework that posits that multiple social categories (e.g., race, ethnicity, gender, sexual orientation, socioeconomic status) intersect at the **micro** level of individual experience to reflect multiple interlocking systems of privilege and oppression at the

macro, social-structural level (e.g., racism, sexism, heterosexism, compulsory heterosexuality, **heteronormativity**, ableism).

We begin here by returning to and expanding on the point previously, that intersectionality is at the heart of feminist analysis, or what Patrick Grzanka calls a "leading paradigm" and an "indispensible tool" (xiii). This fact has a history that is important to recount here, at least briefly. Early models of intersectional analyses of race and gender have been offered by African American women writers dating back to the 19th century (see, e.g., Beverly Guy Sheftall's collection, *Words of Fire*). Sojourner Truth's powerful and foundational 1851 speech to the Women's Convention in Ohio, for example, is suggestive of an intersectional approach:

> That man over there says that women need to be helped into carriages, and lifted over ditches, and to have the best place everywhere. Nobody ever helps me into carriages, or over mud-puddles, or gives me any best place! And ain't I a woman? Look at me! Look at my arm! I have ploughed and planted, and gathered into barns, and no man could head me! And ain't I a woman? I could work as much and eat as much as a man—when I could get it—and bear the lash as well! And ain't I a woman? I have borne thirteen children, and seen most all sold off to slavery, and when I cried out with my mother's grief, none but Jesus heard me! And ain't I a woman?

What Truth aimed to critique were assumptions about womanhood and femininity, and what her speech gets at is the ways that, in the mid-19th century as in contemporary society, womanhood has no single, monolithic definition; race, class, sexuality, and other identities are profound influences on an individual woman's experience, but that all of these rich identities are equally valid forms of womanhood. Intersectionality must be an important consideration when attempting to define, understand, and advocate for the needs of "women."

Intersectionality as a central, formal, and scholarly concern of the field of Women's and Gender Studies did not come about until the late 20th century, and was a result of the powerful critiques leveled by U.S. women of color against some elements of second-wave feminism. Many of these critiques had their origins in the experiences of women who struggled to reconcile their involvement in both antiracist and feminist activism. Latina women, for example, decried the sexism they experienced from Latino men, even as they themselves experienced racism when organizing with white women against sexism. This double bind was succinctly captured by the title of a classic anthology, *All the Women Are White, All the Blacks Are Men, But Some of Us Are Brave: Black Women's Studies*. Many Black and Chicana women, personally faced with both racism and sexism, carved out a middle ground in which they maintained the importance of working in solidarity with men of their racial group. As Elizabeth Martinez writes in "La Chicana," "We will not win our liberation struggle unless the women move together with the men rather than against them. We must work to convince the men that our struggle will become stronger if women are not limited to a few, special roles. We also have the right to expect that our most enlightened men will join the fight against sexism; it should not be our battle alone" (115). On a similar note, the Combahee River Collective writes, "We struggle together with black men against racism, while we also struggle with black men about sexism" (118).

In addition to sometimes facing overt discrimination, a variety of women, including women of color, lesbians, and working-class women, found that their experiences and perspectives were not always reflected in the agendas of feminist organizations, nor reflected in early feminist theorizing. For example, working-class women (both white women and women of color) rightly critiqued the liberal feminist assumption that working outside the home was a key to women's liberation; these women countered that women of their economic class had been working outside the home for generations in ways that had not transformed their experience of sexism, nor had it alleviated their economic struggles. In short, these women revealed the implicit classed assumptions of some liberal feminist agendas, and they challenged feminists to incorporate the perspectives of poor and working-class women into their work. As bell hooks writes in "Rethinking the Nature of Work," some white middle-class feminists in the early second wave "were so blinded by their own experiences that they ignored the fact that a vast majority of women were . . . already working outside the home, working in jobs that neither liberated them from dependence on men nor made them economically self-sufficient" (95). Some conceptions of second-wave feminism, for example, consider Betty Friedan's *Feminine Mystique* to be a touchstone text that relaunched feminist critique of women's social roles. Friedan's illustration of the frustrated ambitions of educated, middle-class women, however, while driving some feminist movement, did not reflect or speak to women who already worked in factories, as domestics, or in service positions, and who felt neither liberated nor empowered by wage work.

Women of color, working-class women, and lesbians were critiquing what Chela Sandoval has called **hegemonic feminism**: that is, a feminism that was "white led, marginalize[d] the activism and world views of women of color, focuse[d] mainly on the United States, and treat[ed] sexism as the ultimate oppression" (Thompson 56). Rather than abandoning feminism, however, women of color, working-class women, and lesbians asserted their right to claim and expand its focus. Barbara Smith, an African American lesbian feminist from a working-class background, coined an expanded, reconfigured definition of feminism that succinctly articulates this critique of and challenge to hegemonic feminism: "Feminism is the political theory and practice to free all women: women of color, working-class women, poor women, physically challenged women, lesbians, old women—as well as white economically privileged heterosexual women. Anything less than this is not feminism, but merely female self-aggrandizement" (48). In this way, intersectionality can be seen as part of the evolution of feminist thinking and action; as the social and political activities surrounding feminist movement matured and gained more ground, so, too, did the focus of feminist theory, and a greater level of alignment between feminist ideals and feminist practice developed.

One way to better understand intersectionality is by exploring what it is *not*, that is, what it stands in contrast to. As a theoretical framework and an analytical approach, intersectionality stands in contrast to a single-lens or single-axis approach. Going back to our opening illustration about Gabby Douglas, a single-lens approach to thinking about Douglas's experience at the Olympics would focus solely on her experience as a woman *or* as an African-American. Grzanka writes, "'Single-axis' is the term used in intersectional research to denote those perspectives, methods, and modes of analysis that privilege one dimension of inequality (e.g., race *or* gender *or* class) and which derive ideas, knowledge, and policy from that single dimension such that all members of a racial, gender, or class group are thought to have essentially the same experiences of race, gender, or class" (xv). But acknowledging that a single lens is insufficient doesn't just mean adding in another separate lens, what Elizabeth Spelman calls an "additive" approach to understanding multiple social categories. In an additive approach, sex and race and class are treated as separate categories, as opposed to intersecting. The Combahee River Collective make this point succinctly when they use the term "simultaneity" to capture the interconnectedness of their identities and oppressions. They write, "We know that there is such a thing as racial-sexual oppression which is neither solely racial nor solely sexual, e.g., the history of rape of Black women by white men as a weapon of political repression" (108). As Richard Delgado and Jean Stefancic concur in their primer, *Critical Race Theory*, "These categories . . . can be separate disadvantaging factors. What happens when an individual occupies more than one of these categories, for example, is both gay and Native American, or both female and Black? Individuals like these operate at an intersection of recognized sites of oppression. Do such cases require that each disadvantaging factors be considered separately, additively, or in some other fashion?" (57) By now we hope it is clear that an intersectional approach requires us to consider them as overlapping, and that without that perspective, we can't fully understand how multiple identities overlap to shape women's experiences on the individual and institutional level.

Having given a sense of why and how intersectionality as a framework and tool came about and what it stands in contrast to, it is also important to briefly sketch out a few examples of what it can *do*, or rather what can be seen and understood when adopting it as a lens or category of analysis.

One of the pioneering texts on the topic of intersectionality is legal scholar Kimberlé Crenshaw's essay "Mapping the Margins: Intersectionality, Identity Politics, and Violence against Women of Color." Crenshaw's particular issue of interest is violence against women. What she illustrates is how an intersectional approach can support social justice by acknowledging that "woman" is not an essential, stable category, and all women who are in violent situations do not face the same challenges or have the same resources. Recognizing, for example, that the role of social class and access to economic resources is of profound importance for women seeking to leave a violent situation, or that national status/immigration status shapes the needs of immigrant women who experience violence, Crenshaw's analysis points to the ways that institutions, as they intersect with individual women's needs, must be examined if we hope to have a full understanding of how to combat racism, sexism, or other forms of social oppression.

Thinking about the issue of combating gendered violence at the level of praxis, without an intersectional approach, a shelter for victims of violence might not consider the need to ensure that their facility was accessible via public transportation so that it could be reached by a wide range of people, not just those who had the economic means to own and/or have access to a car. Similarly, without an intersectional approach, the same shelter might not consider the need to provide their written materials in multiple languages, not just English. And finally, without an intersectional approach, a shelter might not consider that some women seeking their services might be in same-sex relationships, and that some people seeking their services might not be women.

At the level of analysis, intersectionality is also an invaluable tool for making sense of the world around us and for complicating our thinking and understanding. For example, 1970s research about men's gender role expectations by David and Brannon (and popularized by Michael Kimmel) identified four dictates of masculinity: (1) No Sissy Stuff (i.e., a prohibition on expression of feminine characteristics); (2) Be a Big Wheel (i.e., strive for status and success); (3) Be a Sturdy Oak (i.e., be confident, stoic, and self-reliant); and (4) Give 'em Hell (i.e., take risks, be daring and aggressive). If we take a new look at these four dictates of masculinity from an intersectional perspective, we might ask the question of whether and how some of these dictates also have a basis in, or association with, men of different races or classes in ways that don't fully account for men's experiences of male gender socialization. The status and success associated with being a Big Wheel, for example, is clearly defined in terms of material goods and affluence, more typical of a middle-class and upper-middle-class masculinity grounded in consumer capitalism. In other words, we would not be content to think about masculinity exclusively in terms of gender but would ask how race and class, for example, shape its expression. We might also ask whether there are internal tensions or even contradictions in the performance of masculinity that are related to race and class.

One arena in which to try out these ideas would be in the media coverage of male heads of state. Arguably, male heads of state epitomize the second dictate of masculinity, the Big Wheel, but the activities, clothes, and mannerisms that go along with that aspect of masculinity run the risk of overshadowing or perhaps undermining the fourth dictate ("Give 'em Hell"), and also the first, "No Sissy Stuff." Thinking about masculinity in this way can help us understand why Vladimir Putin of Russia so frequently appears shirtless in rugged natural settings; why President George W. Bush was photographed so frequently during his presidency wearing Western-style clothing while engaged in manual labor on his ranch and grabbing a beer with constituents in rural bars; or why President Obama felt compelled to respond publicly and repeatedly to journalists and critics who dubbed the pants he wore to the 2009 Major League Baseball All-Star game "mom jeans." Writing in the *Washington Post* about the "mom jeans" episode, Robin Givhan reflects on the difficulties faced by all campaigning politicians: "When they're angling for votes, they know any hint of rarefied tastes or an aesthetic sensibility that is more Barneys New York than Macy's raises questions about whether they are fit for the job of representing all the regular folks. When it comes to clothes, the president must appear to be as mass market and main floor as possible." Givhan's remarks hint at the class tensions in the president's appearance, but the gender dynamic evident in the descriptor of his jeans is evident as well. The ways that masculinity is classed and racialized will be discussed again in the "Language, Images, and Symbols" anchoring topic.

Learning Roadblock

"We're all different but equal." When introducing the concept of intersectionality to undergraduate students, we find that they are readily able to grasp the notion that the experiences and perspectives of women differ in relation to various additional aspects of identity, and they generally

need look no further than their fellow classmates to understand this. For example, lesbian students immediately grasp that their experience of navigating their social world differs from that of their heterosexual peers; white students acknowledge that the experiences of students of color differ dramatically from theirs; and students from impoverished and working-class backgrounds know from the start that their lives have differed from their middle-class peers in fundamental ways that shape their perspectives on a wide number of issues. In other words, it is relatively easy for students to "get" that it is inaccurate to assume that there is some monolithic set of experiences that are shared by all women.

While this way of understanding intersectionality can be a productive entry point, it is not meant to be an end point. More specifically, the challenge is to think about those differences among women in the context of systems of privilege and oppression (see Chapter 3). Otherwise, we lapse into relativism and lose sight of the significance or implications of those differences in terms of power and privilege.

Learning Roadblock

"Intersectionality is just or only about personal identity." In addition, while intersectionality is relatively easy to understand at a micro level, it is also important to understand the "macro" level of how systems of oppression intersect and are interlocking. The example of immigrant women and intimate partner violence is illustrative here. For example, Crenshaw observes that the provisions in the Immigration Act of 1990 allowed for exceptions to the standard "marriage fraud rules," requiring that immigrant women be married for two years before being considered for permanent citizenship; this made immigrant women particularly vulnerable to battering and abuse because they (a) feared deportation, (b) may have possessed limited language or literacy skills that would prevent them from accessing the resources and securing the documentation required to pursue the exemption process, and (c) face cultural barriers that might discourage women from proceeding with the process. In this case, intersecting institutions—government and legal agencies, family structures, cultural norms, employment status, legal status, marriage structures—all overlap to shape individual women's experiences; simultaneously, immigrant women's language status,

age, class, and national identity make up "micro" categories that are also important in understanding—and interrogating—essentialist rhetorics around equality of choice and autonomy.

With regard to both of these learning roadblocks, the key is to remember that intersectionality is not just (or only) about identity. As Patrick Grzanka points out, "While intersectionality helps us to explore social and personal identities in complex and nuanced ways, intersectional analyses direct their critical attention to categories, structures, and systems that produce and support multiple *dimensions of difference*" (xv). A feminist stance offers us macro-level and critical perspectives on how institutions and other social structures create and maintain these differences—with varying impacts on people affected by them, which is to say, all of us.

Closely related to the issue of what intersectionality, as a tool or lens, can *do*, then, are its goals, or what it aims to accomplish. Dill and Zambrana identify four main goals of intersectional scholarship: "1) reformulate the world of ideas so that it incorporates the many contradictory and overlapping ways that human life is experienced; 2) convey this knowledge by rethinking curricula and promoting institutional change in higher education institutions; 3) apply the knowledge in an effort to create a society in which all voices are heard; and 4) advocate for public policies that are responsive to multiple voices" (177).

Anchoring Topics through the Lens of Intersectionality

Work and Family

Work–life balance refers to the relationship between the policies and lived experiences of working families, particularly those who are managing the demands of paid labor, with the demands of personal and work responsibilities, including children and eldercare. Different countries take different approaches to developing policies that will support this kind of balance—paid family leave to accommodate the birth or adoption of a child or care of a sick family member, for example—as well as policies to support breastfeeding, to accommodate family responsibilities, to care for sick children, or to limit maximum work hours per week. Understanding this issue, however, can be enriched by looking at how social identities as well as institutional practices overlap to create a wide range of policy needs and practices that differ from person to person and within social environments.

In this section, we examine how an intersectional approach is illustrated by the issue of work–life balance, and how to develop a complex understanding of this issue. These are certainly not exclusive in framing discussions of the topic, but they help to illustrate how acknowledging particular identities—such as national origin, social class, race, and marital status—can provide a sharper and more nuanced understanding of this social issue for women.

National Identity

Notably, one of the most critical factors in shaping a woman's experience of work–life balance, particularly her ability to balance paid work with the responsibilities of children or other dependent family members, is the availability of paid family leave. The United States, for example, is one of the least flexible and generous in this area, when compared with industrialized and even developing nations across the globe. As the International Labour Organization documents, more than 120 countries around the world provide paid family leave to accommodate the birth or adoption of a child or the care of a sick relative. As McGill University researchers explain in their report, *The Work, Family, and Equity Index*, 169 of 173 countries studied guarantee some form of paid leave to women in connection with childbirth. Nearly 100 offer at least three months of leave. However, the United States offers no guaranteed paid leave, although up to 12 weeks of unpaid leave is guaranteed by the Family and Medical Leave Act (FMLA) passed in 1993. Other countries that do not offer any form of paid leave include Liberia, Papua New Guinea, and Swaziland (Heymann, Earle, and Hayes 1–2). Another 66 countries offer paid paternal leave. This act also allows for unpaid leave to cover serious illness or the care of a sick family member. The Department of Labor notes that less than half of employers are covered by FMLA—44.2% under the established guidelines.

Women who live in countries with paid leave that cover childbirth, illness, and support breastfeeding as well as the ability to care for dependents and family members who are ill have greater advantages in health and economics than those women who do not have access

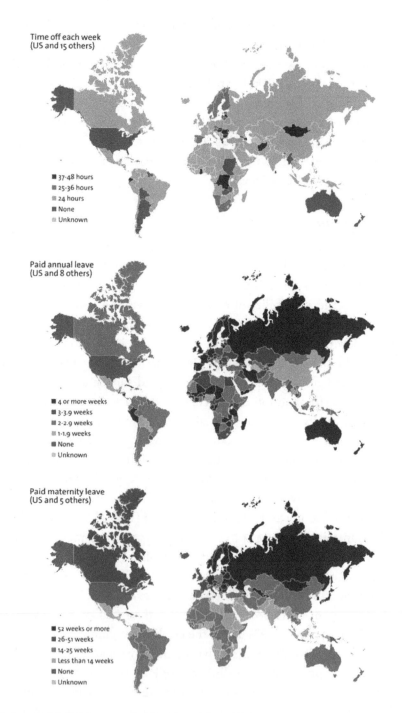

Time off each week
(US and 15 others)

■ 37-48 hours
■ 25-36 hours
▥ 24 hours
■ None
▦ Unknown

Paid annual leave
(US and 8 others)

■ 4 or more weeks
■ 3-3.9 weeks
■ 2-2.9 weeks
▥ 1-1.9 weeks
■ None
▦ Unknown

Paid maternity leave
(US and 5 others)

■ 52 weeks or more
■ 26-51 weeks
■ 14-25 weeks
▥ Less than 14 weeks
■ None
▦ Unknown

Figure 4.2 McGill Institute for Health and Social Policy

to these benefits. Heymann, Earle, and Hayes show that breastfeeding and sufficient post-childbirth bonding time for newborns improves health outcomes, reduces infant mortality rates, and fosters the emotional development of children. Such leave policies also offer economic benefits by stabilizing long-term employability of working families and minimizing the wage gap that working mothers experience (6). As the International Labour Organization explains, "women provide the main source of income in some 30 per cent of all households," and in Europe, "59 percent of working women supply half or more of their family's household income" (International Labour Organization). Without appropriate policies and practices in place that allow women to balance their caregiving responsibilities with paid labor, there are serious economic impacts on working families.

Social Class

Social class and socioeconomic status are profoundly important in shaping women's experiences of the labor market and the various kinds of privileges and rights they are entitled to. Even within certain classes of employment—for example, professional work—there are varying levels of work–life balance and policies that guarantee those. Women working part time, for hourly wages, or in low-income occupations face particular challenges in securing paid leave and time off to accommodate family responsibilities, the birth of a child, or to cover sickness or the illness of a family member. The current FMLA eligibility policies, for example, disproportionately limit the access of part-time and low-income women to its provisions. For example, FMLA applies only to private employers with at least 50 employees, which excludes employees who work for small businesses. It also only applies to those employees who have been working close to full time (1,250 hours/year) and for at least 12 months. For women whose caretaking responsibilities require them to work limited or part-time hours, federal policies are inadequate, such that policies aimed only at "working women" miss an important opportunity to carefully assess the diverse needs of women and make appropriate accommodations and interventions.

Professional women in the labor force with what Sylvia Ann Hewlett has called "extreme jobs" may face a double bind—although they may be salaried employees with a relatively greater degree of job security, corporate culture may dissuade such women (and men) from availing themselves of the policies that do exist to accommodate work–life balance. Marissa Meyer, CEO of online search engine Yahoo, provides a case study of this dilemma. Mayer caused public controversy throughout her 2012 pregnancy and childbirth. Prior to giving birth, Mayer told *Fortune*, "'I like to stay in the rhythm of things,' she said. 'My maternity leave will be a few weeks long and I'll work throughout it.'" In response, Kara Nortman, a fellow woman tech entrepreneur and Senior Vice President of Consumer Businesses at CityGrid Media, wrote an impassioned blog post asking Mayer to "take a real maternity leave of some variety!" Nortman wrote: "Whether Marissa realizes it or not, the way she treats maternity leave will serve as an example or an anti-example for all woman looking for a path, for those women who do not want 'to gap' their ambition, but also want to enjoy *being a parent*." Later, Mayer stated at a public event, "The thing that surprised me is that the job is really fun . . . and the baby's been easy. The baby's been way easier than everyone made it out to be. I've been really lucky that way" (Grose). Mayer's decision to double available family leave for new mothers from 8 weeks to 16 weeks, but to prohibit telecommuting and working from home, also engendered public discussion when Yahoo's new policy was announced. The human resources department released a statement arguing "Speed and quality are often sacrificed when we work from home," and "We need to be one Yahoo!, and that starts with physically being together" (Swisher). In Sylvia Hewett's *Off-Ramps and On-Ramps*, she critiques the "male competitive model" that structures work expectations around extreme hours, office "face time," and relentless demands on the time of employees, along with what she calls "cumulative, lockstep careers and a continuous, linear employment history," a model that can derail women employees in their childbearing years without structural and institutional policies that allow for work–life balance, as the debate around Mayer's pregnancy and postpartum work schedule illustrates.

Benefitting from resources and institutional power, Marissa Mayer's array of choices in work–life/work–family balance stands in striking contrast with those women who do not hold jobs in the professional class.

As *Working Mother* magazine reports, the majority of hourly employees (those who have less secure employment and are more likely to work part time), are women, with women making up 61% of the 75 million hourly employees and a median wage of $11.49 per hour (Working Mother). Simultaneously, the average cost of full-time child care for an infant ranges in 2011 from $4,600 per year in Mississippi to $11,700 in Massachusetts. Center-based child care fees for two children were greater than the cost of household expenditures for rent in all 50 states and average mortgage costs in 20 states (Childcare Aware). As policies and practices are formulated amidst public discourse around women's needs for achieving work–life balance, an intersectional approach maintains an appropriate focus on accurately evaluating these needs and responding in ways that will match those needs.

Language, Images, and Symbols

Chapter 3 presented the idea that systems of privilege and oppression play out through the arena of cultural images and representations. One of the ways that the power of a dominant group manifests is through its ability to produce and control images and representations not only of their own group but of marginalized groups, who by definition have less power. A substantial body of feminist scholarship has focused on the creation and perpetuation of feminine beauty ideals and masculine body ideals. This scholarship has focused on the fact that the cultural images and representations of feminine beauty ideals are often not created by women themselves. Feminist communication and media studies scholarship seeks to explain how the beauty and body ideal functions in the context of consumer capitalism for both men and women. A related focus of feminist scholarship has been the exploration of how people both internalize and resist these images and representations.

An intersectional approach to masculine and feminine norms of appearance emphasizes that those norms differ by race and class. That is, gendered norms of appearance are racialized and classed. Theorist R. W. Connell, for example, writes about "multiple masculinities: black as well as white, working-class as well as middle-class" (256). The popular and controversial reality television show "Duck Dynasty" provides a good example of how masculinity is classed, and more generally shows the socially constructed and performative aspects of masculinity. The hair and clothing of the men featured on the show have become iconic in American culture: consumer products everywhere feature the clan with long hair and beards, wearing camouflage clothing. Photos of the men surfaced in 2012, however, which revealed that prior to their show, they performed masculinity very differently, wearing polo shirts and khaki shorts, with short haircuts and clean cut faces. One photo features the men posed with golf clubs. The outrage some expressed after these photos surfaced came from a sense that the men on the show were attempting to appeal to their largely politically conservative, working-class and male audience through being inauthentic, performing a working-class masculinity that drew from recreational activities (hunting, for example) and male-dominated institutions (military-inspired appearances) to create a hugely profitable popular culture product. At the very least, the two sets of images reveal that masculinity is not monolithic or one-size-fits-all, but rather co-constructed with other aspects of identity and that individuals or groups may and can choose to express those gender constructions differently. Complicating this point, however, is the notion that gender constructions can be wielded for commercial and/or political purposes.

Furthermore, Connell and others have emphasized that some forms of masculinity are valued more highly than others; this point builds on Chapter 2's discussion of gender ranking. Just as masculinity is valued more highly than femininity in our culture, so some forms of masculinity are valued more highly than others. For example, Connell asserts, "Gay men are subordinated to straight men by an array of quite material practices" (257). Paul Kivel makes a similar point when he asserts that while the act-like-a-man box (discussed in Chapter 2) "is a metaphor for the pressure all boys must respond to, the possibility that a boy will have control over the conditions of his life varies depending on his race, class, and culture" (149). Returning to the arena of images and symbols, working-class men and men of color are frequently pathologized in popular culture representations of them, and gay men are frequently represented in stereotypical and one-dimensional ways.

For example, men of color occupy central roles in particular types of popular culture—athletics, particularly football and basketball and to a lesser degree baseball—high status and well-compensated cultural venues that resonate with the "big wheel" and "no sissy stuff" dictates of masculinity. However, male athletes of color must simultaneously occupy a space in which this violent masculinity is particularly fraught because of the intersection of gender and race. For example, the 2014 controversy over remarks made by Seattle Seahawks cornerback Richard Sherman illustrates this dilemma. Following a game-winning play, Sherman conducted a postgame interview with white female sports reporter Erin Andrews, in which he offered comments filled with a range of emotion. Sherman's intense interview resulted in widespread Internet and media characterization of him as a "thug," a term Sherman astutely deconstructed in later interviews, observing "The only reason it bothers me is because it seems like it's the accepted way of calling somebody the N-word nowadays. Because they know" (Petchesky). Although Sherman's remarks to Andrews used the typical athletic rhetoric of dominance (against an opposing team player), Sherman's "outburst" drew a heated public response in which an analysis of television discourse the following day revealed the term "thug" to have appeared three times as frequently as the day before (Wagner). Although Sherman's outburst was hardly more extreme than those that white players offer with regularity, the cultural response supports Greg Howard's claim that "Too many of us think that one ecstatic, triumphant black man showing honest, *human* emotion just seconds after making a play that very well could be written into the first appositive of his obituary, is not only offensive, but is also representative of the tens of millions of blacks in this country. And in two weeks time, in the year 2014, too many of us will be rooting for the Denver Broncos for no other reason than to knock Richard Sherman down a few notches, if only to put him back in his place" (Howard). Many of those criticizing Sherman's behavior and calling him a thug seemed to do so because they perceived his words and actions to be an affront to Erin Andrews's white womanhood (in one highly publicized tweet, her reaction was described as "petrified"). In other words, an intersectional analysis of Sherman's racialized masculinity must be understood in relation to Andrews's racialized femininity.

An intersectional approach to representations of the feminine beauty ideal focuses on the fact that beauty, at least in mainstream, mass-market culture, continues to be defined primarily as white, able-bodied, young, and heterosexual. This means that older women, women of color, women with disabilities, and queer women are featured less often in advertisements, on television, in movies, and on magazine covers. In 1978, Tuchman and colleagues coined the term **symbolic annihilation** to describe the relative absence of marginalized groups in the mass media. This absence has the effect of sending the message that these marginalized groups are unimportant and beneath notice. With regard to beauty ideals, the message is that women who are not white, able-bodied, young, and heterosexual are not attractive or desirable. For example, in their 2006 study of bridal magazines, Frisby and Engstrom asked the question, "How often and in what roles are African American women represented as brides and bridesmaids in advertisements in national bridal magazines over the past five years?" (11–12) They looked at over 6,000 ads in 57 issues of three different bridal magazines and found that less than 2% of the ads featured an African American woman as a bride, and no issues featured an African American bride on its cover, although African Americans make up 13.1% of the U.S. population (U.S. Census). Feminist scholars engaged in this kind of inquiry pose and investigate these questions in order to make visible such gaps in mass media, popular culture, or other forms of symbolic representation.

Furthermore, when women whose identities place them de facto outside the feminine beauty ideal *are* represented in the media, those representations tend to be stereotypical and to reinforce the dominant culture's ideas about these marginalized groups. Women of color and poor women in particular tend to be represented in ways that reinforce their otherness. For example, Patricia Hill Collins has written about the "controlling images" of African American women; in *Black Feminist Thought* she writes, "Portraying African-American women as stereotypical mammies, matriarchs, welfare recipients, and hot mommas helps justify U.S. Black women's oppression. Challenging these controlling images has long been a core theme in Black feminist thought" (69). Vivyan Adair, a white, female professor of Women's Studies raised by a single mother on welfare, uses similar language. In "Branded with Infamy: Inscriptions of Poverty and Class in the United States," she writes, "The bodies of poor women and children, scarred and mutilated by state-mandated material deprivation and public exhibition, work as spectacles, as patrolling images socializing and controlling bodies within the body politic" (461). Adair's claims are clearly shown in some of the most popular contemporary forms of television entertainment. For example, reality television is a genre where working-class women and women of color frequently appear, but often in negative and stereo-typical ways (think "Here Comes Honey Boo Boo"). One show, VH1's "Charm School" (itself an offshoot of "Flavor of Love" and "Rock of Love," which are similar to "The Bachelor") shows not just that the fem-inine beauty ideal is racialized and classed, but also reveals that there is a hierarchy of femininity, with the femininity of working-class women of all races being denigrated and pathologized. The premise of the show is that the feminine behavior and appearance of the women featured on the show is problematic and dysfunctional; the show offers to teach these women the proper, correct type of femininity, which is to say, a dominant culture (read: white and middle class) femininity.

An intersectional approach to representations of the feminine beauty ideal not only focuses on whether and how diverse groups of women appear in the mass media; it also focuses on how diverse groups of women respond to and are affected by the mainstream culture's narrow construction of beauty. Lisa Duke, for example, notes "the interest media scholars and critics have shown in identifying the ways in which the mass media might be implicated in producing negative psychic effects in women and girls" (367). In her article "Black in a Blonde World: Race and Girls' Interpretations of the Feminine Ideal in Teen Magazines," she set out to explore how "race influence[s] girls' readings of teen magazines and the magazines' portrayals of the feminine ideal" (368).

Media critics interested in an audience's response to a text and whether and how they are affected by it have noted that responses range from accommodation to rejection and all points in between—what Stuart Hall referred to as dominant hegemonic, negotiated, and oppositional readings. In Duke's findings, based on interviews with middle-class white and African American teen girls, the African Amer-ican girls invested less authority in the teen magazines' prescriptions about beauty and body image than the white girls did. When asked, the African American teens defined beauty more often in terms of personality than physical appearance, and valued a different body aesthetic (curvier and heavier) than the white girls did. This is not to say, however, that African American girls and women, as well as other women of color, do not experience self-doubt or lowered self-esteem as a result of their symbolic annihilation in the media, but rather that their relative absence from beauty magazines in particular is a double-edged sword, providing both the message that they are outside the dominant beauty ideal, but also allowing some space for the creation of an alternate ideal. That is to say, there are competing beauty ideals that are community specific, that is, within a lesbian community, various racial-ethnic communities, and so forth. Many women engage simultaneously in acts of accommodation and resistance, choosing to emulate the mainstream beauty ideal in some ways while rejecting other aspects of it.

The work of scholars such as Connell, Hill Collins, Adair, and Duke, among many others, illustrates that questions about the symbolic dimensions of gender are intersected with race and class and not homogeneously connected to critiques of sexism or misogyny in ways that are generalizable to all men and women.

Bodies

The topic of women's reproductive control, particularly the female-controlled hormonal, oral contraceptive, illustrates how an intersectional lens can deepen our understanding of women's sexuality and the multiple identities that inflect it. As the PBS documentary, *The Pill*, explains, one of the early goals of the women's movement, after suffrage, was female-controlled birth control. However, limiting conversations around women's access to birth control overlooks a number of the intragroup differences that shape women's needs: for example, lesbians may have different reproductive needs than heterosexual women; historically, many African American women's concerns had different emphases than white women; women with class privilege had a much larger array of options in terms of birth control and abortion than working-class and working-poor women; and marital status and age were, and continue to be, important in reflecting and determining a woman's reproductive needs and her level of reproductive control.

A look at the historical conditions out of which the female-controlled oral contraceptive emerged provides insight into the way institutions intersect and individual women's identities frame their experiences. Birth control activist Margaret Sanger opened a birth control clinic in the United States in 1916. With the financial backing of wealthy philanthropist Katharine Dexter McCormick, Sanger spearheaded the efforts on contraceptive research, ultimately collaborating with McCormick and scientist Gregory Pincus to explore hormonal birth control methods. An intersectional lens shows that social class played an important role in allowing Sanger and McCormick to advocate for access to female-controlled birth control, as did their respective educational achievements. McCormick had access to higher education; she earned a degree in biology from Massachusetts Institute of Technology—only the second woman to do so. Sanger pursued nursing training as a young woman. Influenced by her social location as the daughter of Irish Catholic parents, Sanger's views on women's material conditions were driven by several key experiences: she was the sixth of 11 children, and her mother had 18 pregnancies in 22 years before dying at age 50. Sanger's father, an atheist and advocate for public education, as well as Sanger's own marriage to architect William Sanger, influenced her progressive views on access to contraception. Her work in immigrant neighborhoods of New York City cemented her views on the critical need for all women to control the timing and spacing of their pregnancies. She frequently saw immigrant and working-class women suffering physical, material, and familial effects of frequent pregnancies, miscarriages, and self-induced abortions. Race, class, and gender intersected here in shaping the varying experiences of women of the era in terms of their access to paid labor, their ability to control their reproductive lives, and their access to contraceptive information and services.

In the development of the pill, two particular features deserve attention in order to illustrate how intersectional approaches can complicate and unpack discussions around reproductive control. Sanger and McCormick led the development of the new technology, but the scientific work was done by Gregory Pincus, and the human trials—required for any such drug—were led by Dr. John Rock. However, given that distributing contraceptives or information about contraceptives was illegal in most places in the United States, Rock sought out another region and population that could participate in the human clinical trials: Puerto Rico. Region and race play roles here in understanding the significance of the pill's development, as Puerto Rican women who participated in the study were typically illiterate or semiliterate and were part of a developing industrial culture that was producing more opportunities for women's employment outside the home. Charges of racial discrimination—or put differently, racial and class exploitation—have been retrospectively alleged regarding this work because of the lack of what we now know as **informed consent**. Participants in modern-day studies such as these would have been required to receive a more substantial education about the potential side effects of the drug and would not have been participants for the length of time that they were. Because of the heavy dosages used in the early versions of the pill, close to 17% of study participants had significant side effects and 25 withdrew because of the seriousness of those effects. One participant died of congestive heart failure. In this instance, participants' identities as working-class Latinas intersected with their gender in the access to social power, information, and protection afforded them during the study process.

Objections from African American Communities

Emerging from past coercive sterilization practices imposed on African American women, controversy about black women's use of the pill complicated the discussion of reproductive control and the development of the oral contraceptive. A story in the *Nation* in 1974 documented multiple cases of coerced sterilization, such as two adolescent sisters who were sterilized after their mother, who was illiterate, was presented with misleading information about the nature of the procedure. Another case reported on the coerced sterilization of Nial Cox, 26, who was told her family would not be eligible for welfare benefits if she did not undergo the procedure. Against this backdrop and in the simultaneous cultural context of the Black Power movement, an outgrowth of the civil rights movement of the 1960s, African American men and women were justifiably suspicious of what they viewed as efforts on the part of whites to limit black fertility. Whereas for many white women the pill heralded a new level of self-determination and autonomy around controlling the timing and spacing of pregnancies, African Americans were concerned that oral contraception was "just another tool in the white man's efforts to curtail the Black population" (Roberts). Simultaneous public debates about the eugenics movement and research agendas focused on documenting the inferiority of immigrants and people of color provided reason for African Americans to believe that racial genocide was part of the explanation for the widespread availability of oral contraceptives. Within the black community, opinions were split, with many African American women welcoming access to a tool for reproductive control; however, African American feminist activists, such as Toni Cade in her 1969 essay "The Pill: Genocide or Liberation?" reflect the conflicted position of some blacks about the motivation and implications of the pill's development. Cade recalled attending an activism meeting in which a "tall, lean dude went into deep knee bends as he castigated the sisters to throw away the pill and hop to the mattresses and breed revolutionaries and mess up the man's genocidal program" (163). Reporting on the strong objections that women workshop attendees expressed, Cade wrote, "while I agree with the need to produce, I don't agree to the irresponsible, poorly thought-out call to young girls, on-the-margins scufflers, every Sister at large to abandon the pill that gives her certain decision power, a power that for a great many of us is all we know, given the setup in this country and in our culture" (164). Acknowledging that she "would never agree that the pill really liberates women. It only helps," Cade acknowledged the lack of resources for women raising children: abysmal family leave policies; gendered divisions of labor around childrearing; abortion fatalities; and employment discrimination as framing the conversation for African American women around the use of the pill.

Such conversations continue even in today's current events and media culture. In July 2013, news reports revealed that between 2006 and 2010 nearly 150 female inmates were subjected to involuntary or coerced sterilization. In rhetoric eerily similar to that used decades earlier in support of eugenics, the prison ob–gyn rationalized the procedures: "Dr. Heinrich denied he pressured anyone into sterilization and said the $147,460 isn't a major cost. Heinrich said the procedures are important because women with a prison history 'procreated more.'" "Over a 10-year period, that isn't a huge amount of money," Heinrich said, "compared to what you save in welfare paying for these unwanted children" (Post Staff Reporters). What this history and ongoing practice reveals is not just the vexed relationship between African American women and birth control, but the critical importance of recognizing multiple identity factors and intragroup differences that will enrich and provide a finer-grained understanding of complex issues like those studied by feminist scholars—in this case, reproductive justice.

Institutional Intersectionality

Although perhaps the most intuitive way to understand intersectionality is to see overlapping identities—sometimes called a confluence—as explaining the different experiences of different people, it's important to recognize that intersectionality and personal experiences are always framed by the social institutions in our lives. On the topic of reproductive control, a number of key institutions influence women's access and resources, and they themselves intersect to grant privileges to some groups and withhold them from others. Institutions at play include the cultural expectations around marriage, the laws and policies that govern access to contraceptive information, and religious doctrine that prohibited women's use of contraceptive technology.

Marriage, both in terms of cultural expectations about marriage and its responsibilities, and the laws that governed the level of reproductive control women experienced depending on their marital status both demonstrate how institutions intersect with each other, as access to and information about reproductive technologies were legally limited. For example, the Comstock Act was an 1873 "antiobscenity law" that defined information about birth control as obscene and outlawed its distribution (*Time*). Margaret Sanger was indicted and arrested under these laws for circulating information about birth control to poor women and for opening a birth control clinic. Even after Comstock Laws were repealed under the obscenity ban, contraception remained illegal in most states.

The influence of marital status and the far reach of institutions in limiting and granting privilege is illustrated by the two court cases that decriminalized contraception. In 1965, the landmark Supreme Court case of **Griswold v. Connecticut** struck down laws that prohibited contraception for married couples. However, it wasn't until the 1972 *Eisenstadt v. Baird* case that unmarried couples were given equal legal protection to the right to purchase and use contraception. Of course, this institutional imprimatur both shaped access and influenced conduct.

Further, religious organizations as institutions held great sway, both formal and informal, over religious women's reproductive lives. Particularly influential in the development and cultural implications of the advent of the hormonal oral contraceptive was the Catholic Church. The mid-20th century was a time of tremendous unrest within the church on the issue of women's reproduction; in 1951 it affirmed its opposition to any form of artificial birth control. In 1964, Pope Paul IV formed the "Papal Commission on Population, the Family, and Natality," referred to as the "Birth Control Permission." This group was charged with exploring the topic of artificial birth control and its consistency with Catholic doctrine. Although the pill was enjoying widespread use by this point—with 6.5 million women using it by 1965—religious authority still held tremendous influence over individual women's choices regarding the use of this new form of birth control. Many Catholics were hopeful that the formation of this group might lead to a reversal of church doctrine on contraception that had been established during the early period after the death of Jesus (Marks 217). As Marks writes, "60 of the 64 theological experts and 9 of the 15 cardinals sitting on the commission favoured a change," observing that "the majority did not see contraception as intrinsically evil, or consider that the church's acceptance of contraception would go against its teachings and tradition" (226). However, in 1968, Pope John Paul, recommitting to the belief that "his views were valueless when weighed against the history of his institution," reaffirmed the church's commitment to prohibiting all forms of contraception, mechanical or chemical. The papal encyclical *Humanae Vitae* asserted: "Consequently, it is a serious error to think that a whole married life of otherwise normal relations can justify sexual intercourse which is deliberately contraceptive and so intrinsically wrong" (Paul VI). Even though the commission recommended otherwise, the pope reasserted the institution's traditional stance more firmly than ever. For Catholic women, about 25% of the U.S. population, the role of their religious institution played a tremendous role in their willingness and ability to use hormonal contraception, and this access was simultaneously shaped by marital status and social class.

Impact of Expanded Reproductive Control in the United States

As Planned Parenthood reports, there has been a significant decline in maternal and infant mortality since the legalization of contraceptive technologies. For example, in 1964, there were 31.6 maternal deaths per 100,000 live births, but that number was reduced to 12.7 in 2007—nearly a 60% drop. Infant mortality shows a similar decline, with the death rate of infants (those less than one year old) dropping from 24.7 per 1,000 live births to 6.39. The ability to control timing between pregnancies is a significant contributor to women's physiological ability to nurture additional pregnancies and care for newborns, both of which significantly tax a woman's physical, mental, family, and financial resources.

Case Study: Breasts

Breastfeeding and Intersectionality: As a public health issue, infant feeding practices are clearly an issue that solely affect women and babies, but public policy discussions that focus only on gender as a lens for understanding the issue will not accurately capture or target the needs of different women. Recent news reports, for example, tout the increase in mothers breastfeeding their newborns, noting "More mothers in the United States are breastfeeding their babies, a practice that could potentially save billions in health care costs, the Centers for Disease Control said in a study released on Wednesday" (Abutaleb). Aggregate data from the Centers for Disease Control and Prevention (CDC) show, for example, that "While 35 percent of babies were breastfed at six months in 2000, that figure climbed to 49 percent in 2010, and the 27 percent of babies still breastfeeding at 12 months was up from 16 percent over that same decade" (Abutaleb).

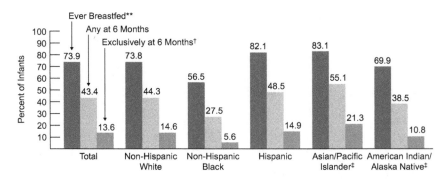

Figure 4.3 Infants* Who Are Breastfed, by Race/Ethnicity and Duration, 2006

Centers for Disease Control and Prevention, National Immunization Survey

*Includes only infants born in 2006; data are provisional. **Reported that child was ever breastfed or fed human breastmilk. †Exclusive breastfeeding is defined as only human breastmilk—no solids, water, or other liquids. ‡Includes Hispanics.

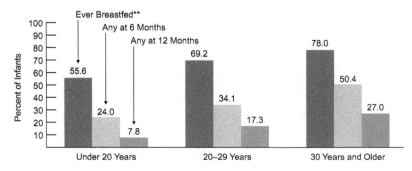

Figure 4.4 Infants* Who Are Breastfed, by Maternal Age and Duration, 2006

Centers for Disease Control and Prevention, National Immunization Survey

*Includes only infants born in 2006; data are provisional. **Reported that child was ever breastfed or fed human breastmilk.

However, an intersectional analysis that examines breastfeeding will acknowledge that race, class, and age as lenses present a more nuanced picture of infant feeding practices and potential public health initiatives. For example, data from the CDC show that factors such as race,

	Breastfeeding Rate in Hospital			Breastfeeding Rate 6 Months After Birth		
	1991	2002	Change	1991	2002	Change
Maternal age (yrs)						
<20	32.2	56.2	24.0	5.9	16.7	10.8
20–24	45.7	66.0	20.3	11.4	25.4	14.0
25–29	57.8	73.4	15.6	19.7	35.7	16.0
30–34	65.2	76.4	11.2	27.3	42.3	15.0
≥35	66.7	74.1	7.4	32.9	43.1	10.2
Maternal education						
Grade school	35.2	55.1	19.9	12.6	27.1	14.5
High school	42.9	60.7	17.8	12.2	23.4	11.2
Non-college	42.6	60.5	17.9	12.2	23.5	11.3
College	70.2	81.2	11.0	27.7	44.6	16.9
Unknown	N/A	N/A		N/A	N/A	
Race/ethnicity						
Hispanic	51.8	70.7	18.9	14.8	32.7	17.9
Non-Hispanic, Black	25.8	53.9	28.1	6.6	19.2	12.6
Non-Hispanic, White	59.2	73.4	14.2	21.0	36.0	15.0
Other	N/A	N/A		N/A	N/A	
Census division						
New England	55.9	73.3	17.4	19.7	37.0	17.3
Middle Atlantic	48.3	65.5	17.2	16.8	33.2	16.4
East North Central	48.8	66.7	17.9	16.6	28.7	12.1
West North Central	56.4	73.1	16.7	18.9	35.2	16.3
South Atlantic	46.4	67.5	21.1	14.5	31.2	16.7
East South Central	37.5	57.0	19.5	10.7	22.0	11.3
West South Central	48.4	64.9	16.5	14.0	27.3	13.3
Mountain	70.0	81.0	11.0	28.0	40.5	12.5
Pacific	69.5	81.5	12.0	25.7	43.4	17.7

Figure 4.5 U.S. Breastfeeding Rates by Selected Characteristics, 1991 and 2002

Jacknowitz, Alison. "Increasing Breastfeeding Rates: Do Changing Demographics Explain Them?" *Women's Health Issues.* 17 (2006): 84–92.

Notes: Data are from Abbott Laboratories (2001, 2002). Breastfeeding rates are unavailable for mothers with unknown education or other race/ethnicity.

educational attainment, and socioeconomic status intersect with gender to reveal trends in breastfeeding. Review the following data table from the CDC's "Infant Feeding Practices" Survey and determine (a) which static factors make it most likely that a mother will choose breastfeeding; and (b) which dynamic factors (changeable factors) make it most likely that a mother will choose breastfeeding.

Questions for Consideration

- Based on these data, what conclusions do you draw about the identity factors that shape mother's infant feeding practices?
- How are women's choices about whether and how long to breastfeed possibly shaped by their experiences of oppression and/or privilege? What material circumstances and conditions (at home, at work, and in public spaces) would ideally enable a woman to breastfeed should she desire to do so?
- Conversely, what circumstances and conditions (at home, at work, and in public spaces) would constrain her ability to do so?
- What points of interest do you observe in this data? What are potential policy implications?
- If you were a part of a team designing a public health campaign to encourage women to breastfeed for the first six months of a baby's life, how could you make sure that your messages of encouragement took issues of race and class into account? What would those messages consist of?

Breast Cancer and Intersectionality

Considerable public, medical, and media attention has been paid in the last two decades to treating and finding a cure for breast cancer. Even though some men are affected by breast cancer, most of the campaigns, such as the Susan G. Komen Race for the Cure and the various "Pink Ribbon" campaigns to support breast cancer research, are gendered feminine and employ a single-axis lens. However, an approach to the issue of breast cancer prevention, diagnosis, treatment, and prevention that uses an intersectional lens will better meet the needs of all women.

Breast cancer survivor rates that are aggregated are grouped by the stage of diagnosis, such as this chart from the American Cancer Society:

Table 4.1 Breast Cancer Survivor Rate By Stage

Stage	5-year Survival Rate
0	100%
I	100%
II	93%
III	72%
IV	22%

However, a closer examination of breast cancer incidences of diagnosis and mortality rates using an intersecting lens of race and gender reveals stark differences. For example, research published in the *Journal of the American Medical Association* showed that black women had a significantly lower five-year survival rate than white women, 55.9% versus 68.8%, when being diagnosed with similar cancer characteristics (Silber, et al.). Further, black women had longer delays in treatment, and were less than half as likely to initiate treatment within three months of diagnosis, with 82% of white women starting treatment within 30 days compared with 69% of black women (U.S. Department of Health and Human Services). CDC research confirms that "Black women experience higher death rates even though they have a lower incidence of breast cancer compared to white women," a disparity that some have explained through inequities at all stages of the medical processes, from screening to diagnosis to treatment. For example, research studies have confirmed that black women are more likely to have more aggressive disease, more advanced disease at the time of diagnosis, a higher incidence of obesity, and higher rates of other illnesses (Penner, et al.).

A number of factors have been identified in an effort to explain *why* these disparities exist and how they play out. For example, Penner and colleagues propose that effective information exchanges during medical consults with oncologists is a critical point of disparity. When patient and doctor have a shared understanding of the information that was exchanged, Penner and colleagues characterize that as "high convergence"; interactions are "low convergence" when patient–doctor understanding is limited. Research suggests that "there are racial/ethnic disparities in the quality of exchange of information in oncology interactions"; for example, 'question-asking frequency,' or the degree to which patients ask for definitions, clarifications, or elaboration on information, contributes to a high convergence rate. However, as Eggly and colleagues conclude, "Blacks asked fewer questions per interaction, and the proportion of direct questions was significantly smaller among Black than White patients" (quoted in Penner et al. 335). Other proposed explanations for gaps in treatment and survival rates include the following:

- variance in the quality of health insurance: According to Penner and colleagues (citing Smedley, et al.), private insurance coverage typically produces better-quality health care access; 71% percent of whites have such coverage in contrast to 54% of blacks.
- some research (Barnato et al. 2005) shows that black patients are disproportionately served by "hospitals that had lower rates of evidence-based medical treatments, higher rates of cardiac procedures, and worse risk-adjusted mortality after acute myocardial infarction (quoted in Penner et al. 345).
- patient perception: Research shows that black patients are more likely to be mistrustful of white physicians and healthcare systems more broadly than white patients. As Halbert and colleagues discovered in their study, "Racial Differences in Trust in Health Care Providers," in *Archives of Internal Medicine*: "Consistent with previous research, African Americans were significantly more likely than whites to report low trust in health care providers in this study. Even after controlling for socio-demographics, prior health care experiences, and structural characteristics of care, African American race had a significant effect on low trust" (899).

An intersectional approach to gender issues focused on medical and public health questions such as these can help illuminate how issues that may on the surface seem homogeneous are actually complex and nuanced and may require parsing out factors around identity that can more effectively help us understand, target, and act on inequities or disparities.

End of Chapter Elements

Evaluating Prior Knowledge

1. What previous uses have you heard of the term "intersections" or "intersect"? What other commonplace uses are there of these terms? What connotations or associations do you have with the term? Do these associations help you think more about this discipline-specific use of the term? In other words, how do those "common-sense" understandings of intersections help to amplify, elaborate, or illuminate your understanding of the material in this chapter?

2. Consider previous learning you've done in an educational context on gender, women, or power and privilege. Can you identify any course materials, readings, lectures, or topics that used an intersectional approach? If not, explain how your learning about that topic would have been enriched by using an intersectional lens.

Application Exercises

1. Consider the following list of topics that are considered "women's issues" (do some Internet research to learn more about any that are unfamiliar to you)
    a. abortion rights
    b. "staying at home" versus working outside the home at paid employment
    c. violence against women
    d. emergency contraception or access to "Plan B"
    e. equal pay/the wage gap
    f. female genital cutting
    g. the medicalization of childbirth
    h. *maquiladoras*
    i. eating disorders, media, and beauty ideals
    j. women and political representation

    Next, select one of these issues and try to apply an "intersectional" lens to key questions, concerns, or debates within and about that issue. For example, although certainly all of these issues affect women, are there ways that race, social class, sexual orientation, or national origin complicate these issues or are reflected in different ways depending on how multiple identities are considered as part of the analysis?

2. Returning to the opening illustration about the 2012 Olympics, briefly research Castor Semenya and the debates that emerged around sex, gender expression, and gender identity as well as the controversies around Olympic sex tests. In what ways does Semenya's story lend itself to an intersectional approach, particularly relating to gender, race, and national identity?

3. Watch this video developed by NBC during the 2012 Olympics and commented on by feminist media site Jezebel: http://jezebel. com/5933302/someone-at-nbc-apparently-approved-this-creepy-porny-video-of-female-olympians. In what ways does Jezebel commentator Erin Gloria Ryan use an intersectional lens to critique the video? In what ways would you add an intersectional critique to the video?

4. Research the 2011 decision to prohibit the Iranian women's soccer team from competing in an Olympic qualifying match because the players wore the *hijab*, the traditional Muslim head covering. Subsequent Olympic events have loosened the strictures on female Muslim athletes' donning of headscarves while competing, but not without significant controversy. What intersecting identities are at work in this historical and nationally significant athletic competition and women's participation in it?

Skills Assessment/Check for Understanding

1. Khalia is a 30-year-old biracial woman (her mother is African American, and her father is from Iran); she was raised in Milwaukee; she was educated at the University of Wisconsin–Madison and then Harvard; she is Muslim; she is a doctor and her family is affluent; she lives in a small, rural Wisconsin town with her husband and two children where she works at the local hospital. Drawing on Peggy McIntosh's article "The Invisible Knapsack," in what ways is Khalia privileged? In what ways is she not

privileged? How does intersectionality apply to Khalia and her experiences?

2. An important theoretical tradition in understanding intersectionality theory is Critical Race Theory. Briefly discuss your understanding of each of the following concepts, and cite a relevant current events story, policy decision, or popular culture event that will help illustrate your understanding of each concept.

    a. racism as embedded into the institutions of our society (business, education, the law)
    b. the limits of using a "color blindness" approach to policy and practice
    c. the social construction of race as a category of identity
    d. differential racialization (the way that racial identities shift, even among the same racial groups, according to the historical era and the cultural, historical, and economic contexts of the time and place)

Discussion Questions

1. Consider an area of your own interest or expertise (this could be a hobby, an academic major, or an important cocurricular activity you engage in), and identify an important issue, question, or controversy within that area of interest. How might an intersectional approach that accounts for multiple overlapping identities help you approach that issue? Share your findings with a classmate.

2. Choose a favorite film genre and screen at least three films in that genre. Take note of the number of women characters, the type of women characters, and relevant identity factors—marital status, educational attainment, race, class, sexual orientation. What conclusions can you draw about "women in X genre" of film based on your analysis? Does an intersectional approach help you with that analysis?

Writing Prompts

1. Using your library's database, locate the article "Welfare Policymaking and Intersections of Race, Ethnicity, and Gender in U.S. State Legislatures" by Beth Reingold and Adrienne Smith (*American*

Journal of Political Science, 46.1 (2012), 131–147). Reingold and Smith use an intersectional lens to examine state welfare policy and how influential gender, race, and ethnicity are on shaping legislative policy around welfare reform. Using Reingold and Smith's two proposed approaches—an additive approach and an intersectional approach—examine the diversity of legislative representation in your home state or local community. Consider investigating a particular policy issue as well as how different legislators voted on that policy issue and its outcome. Does an intersectional or additive approach offer insight into the policy questions and outcomes?

2. In her essay, "Mapping the Margins: Intersectionality, Identity Politics, and Violence against Women of Color," Kimberlé Williams Crenshaw writes the following: "The problem with identity politics is not that it fails to transcend difference, as some critics charge, but rather the opposite—that it frequently conflates or ignores intragroup differences . . . Moreover, ignoring difference within groups contributes to tension among groups, another problem of identity politics" (357). Although, as a feminist legal scholar, Crenshaw is particularly interested in the issue of violence against women and women's employment experiences, her foundational idea is that identities are complex and that a number of categories of identity shape our social experiences. Review the following series of connected Department of Justice websites on the issue of violence against tribal women and write an analysis of violence against Native American women using the intersectional lens that Crenshaw describes.

    a. www.ovw.usdoj.gov/tribal.html

    b. www.ovw.usdoj.gov/section904-taskforce.html

    c. Consider also this extensive report on "Violence against American Indian Women and Alaska Native Women and the Criminal Justice System: What Is Known" (www.ncjrs.gov/pdffiles1/nij/grants/223691.pdf) in formulating your response.

3. In 2012, then 15-year-old tennis player Taylor Townsend (an African American female) won the Australian Open junior title and was the top-ranked junior player in the world. Later that same year, however, the U.S. Tennis Association strongly discouraged her from

Figure 4.6 AP Photo/Darko Vojinovic

competing in the U.S. Open Junior Tennis Tournament, citing their
concerns about her lack of physical conditioning. Thinking about
the discussions of "Bodies" in the anchoring topics in this chapter,
consider the following questions: What does her experience reveal
about the racial, gender, and class politics of the sport of women's
tennis? In what ways can you "read" Townsend's experience through
an intersectional lens that considers identity as well as institutional
structures?

4. In June 2013, the World Health Organization released a report
   on the prevalence of physical and sexual violence against women
   globally. Review the key findings of the report "Global and
   Regional Estimates of Violence against Women: Prevalence and
   Health Effects of Intimate Partner Violence and Non-partner
   Sexual Violence"[1] (see Figure 4.7) and conduct an intersectional
   analysis. What identity factors gesture toward or account for wom-
   en's experiences? What policy interventions seem most promising?

PREVALENCE →

1 in 3 women

throughout the world will experience physical and/or sexual violence by a partner or sexual violence by a non-partner

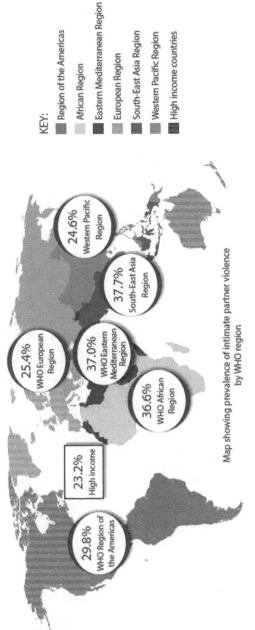

29.8%
WHO Region of the Americas

23.2%
High income

25.4%
WHO European Region

37.0%
WHO Eastern Mediterranean Region

36.6%
WHO African Region

24.6%
Western Pacific Region

37.7%
South-East Asia Region

Map showing prevalence of intimate partner violence by WHO region

KEY:

Region of the Americas

African Region

Eastern Mediterranean Region

European Region

South-East Asia Region

Western Pacific Region

High income countries

Figure 4.7 World Health Organization

Note

1   www.who.int/mediacentre/news/releases/2013/violence_against_women_
    20130620/en/

Works Cited and Suggested Readings

Abutaleb, Yasmeen. "Nudged by Hospitals, More U.S. Moms Are Breastfeeding: CDC."
    Reuters. 31 July 2013. Web.

Adair, Vivyan. "Branded with Infamy: Inscriptions of Poverty and Class in the United
    States." *Signs*. 27.2: 451–471. Print.

Allison, Dorothy. *Skin: Talking about Sex, Class, and Literature*. Ithaca, NY: Firebrand
    Books, 1994. Print.

American Cancer Society. "Survival Rates for Breast Cancer." 4 September 2012. Web.

Anzaldua, Gloria. *Borderlands: La Frontera*. San Francisco: Spinsters/Aunt Lute, 1987.
    Print.

Babcock, Richard. "Sterilization: Coercing Consent." *Nation*. 12 January 1974. Web.

"Breastfeeding." *Women's Health USA*. U.S. Department of Health and Human Services.
    2010. Web.

Cade, Toni. "The Pill: Genocide or Liberation?" In *The Black Woman: An Anthology*. Ed.
    Toni Cade. New York: Signet, 1970. Print.

Carlson, Nicholas. "Marissa Mayer Had a Baby Boy!" *Business Insider*. 1 October 2012.
    Web.

Childcare Aware. *Parents and the High Cost of Childcare*. 2012 Report. 28 July 2013. Web.

Collins, Patricia Hill. "Toward a New Vision: Race, Class, and Gender as Categories
    of Analysis and Connection." *Oppression, Privilege, and Resistance: Theoretical Per-
    spectives on Racism, Sexism, and Heterosexism*. Ed. Lisa Heldke and Peg O'Connor.
    New York: McGraw Hill, 2004. 529–543. Print.

Combahee River Collective, "A Black Feminist Statement." *Feminist Theory Reader:
    Local and Global Perspectives* 3rd ed. Eds. Carole R. McCann and Seung-kyung
    Kim. New York: Routledge, 2013. 116–122. Print.

Connell, Raewyn. "The Social Organization of Masculinity." *Feminist Theory Reader:
    Local and Global Perspectives*. 3rd ed. Eds. Carole R. McCann and Seung-kyung
    Kim. New York: Routledge, 2013. 252–263. Print.

Crenshaw, Kimberlé W. "Mapping the Margins: Intersectionality, Identity Politics, and
    Violence against Women of Color." *Stanford Law Review*. (1991) 43.6: 1241–1299.
    Print.

David, Deborah, and Robert Brannon, eds. *The Forty-Nine Percent Majority: The Male
    Sex Role*. Reading, MA: Addison-Wesley, 1976. Print.

Delgado, Richard, and Jean Stefancic. *Critical Race Theory: An Introduction*. New York:
    New York UP, 2012. Print.

Dill, Bonnie Thornton, and Ruth Enid Zambrana. "Critical Thinking about Inequal-
    ity: An Emerging Lens." *Feminist Theory Reader: Local and Global Perspectives*. 3rd
    ed. Eds. Carole R. McCann and Seung-kyung Kim. New York: Routledge, 2013.
    176–186. Print.

Duke, Lisa. "Black in a Blonde World: Race and Girls' Interpretations of the Feminine
    Ideal in Teen Magazines." *Journalism and Mass Communication Quarterly*. 77.2:
    367–392. Print.

Freedman, Estelle. *No Turning Back: The History of Feminism and the Future of Women*. New York: Ballantine Books, 2002. Print.

Frisby, Cynthia M. and Erika Engstrom. "Always a Bridesmaid, Never a Bride: Portrayals of Women of Color in Bridal Magazines." *Media Report to Women* 34.4 (Fall 2006): 10–14. Print.

Givhan, Robin. "Can Obama Elevate the Look of Presidential Downtime? We Can Only Hope." *Washington Post.* 26 July 2009. Web.

Grose, Jessica. "Why Does the Internet Hate Marissa Mayer's Baby?" *Slate.* 30 November 2012. Web.

Grzanka, Patrick R., ed. *Intersectionality: A Foundations and Frontiers Reader.* Boulder, CO: Westview P, 2014. Print.

Guy-Sheftall, Beverly, ed. *Words of Fire: An Anthology of African-American Feminist Thought.* New York: New Press, 1995. Print.

Halbert, Chanita Hughes, et al. "Racial Differences in Trust in Health Care Providers." *Archives of Internal Medicine.* 166 (April 2006): 396–901. Print.

Hewlett, Sylvia Ann. *Off-Ramps and On-Ramps: Keeping Talented Women on the Road to Success.* Boston, MA: Harvard Business School P, 2007. Print.

Heymann, Jody, Alison Earle, and Jeffrey Hayes. "The Work, Family, and Equity Index: How Does the United States Measure Up?" *McGill University Institute for Health and Social Policy. Project on Global Working Families.* 2008.

Hill Collins, Patricia. *Black Feminist Thought: Knowledge, Consciousness, and the Politics of Empowerment.* New York: Routledge, 1991. Print.

hooks, bell. *Feminist Theory: From Margin to Center.* Boston: South End P, 1984. Print.

Howard, Greg. "Richard Sherman and the Plight of the Conquering Negro." *Deadspin.* 20 January 2014. Web.

Hull, Gloria T., Patricia Bell Scott, and Barbara Smith. *All the Women Are White, All the Blacks Are Men, But Some of Us Are Brave: Black Women's Studies.* New York: The Feminist Press, 1982. Print.

International Labour Organization. "More Than 120 Nations Provide Paid Maternity Leave." 16 February 1998. Web.

Jacknowitz, Alison. "Increasing Breastfeeding Rates: Do Changing Demographics Explain Them." *Women's Health Issues.* 17 (2006): 84–92. Web.

Katharine Dexter McCormick Library. "The Birth Control Pill: A History." *Planned Parenthood.* 15 August 2014. Web.

Marks, Lara. *Sexual Chemistry: A History of the Contraceptive Pill.* New Haven: Yale UP, 2001. Print.

Martinez, Elizabeth. *Feminist Theory Reader: Local and Global Perspectives.* 3rd ed. Eds. Carole R. McCann and Seung-kyung Kim. New York: Routledge, 2013. 113–115. Print.

McCarthy, Sheryl. "Behind the Abortion Color Line." *Nation.* 27 April 2009. Web.

Paul IV. "Encyclical Letter *Humanae Vitae* of the Supreme Pontiff Paul VI to His Venerable Brothers the Patriarchs, Archbishops, Bishops and Other Local Ordinaries in Peace and Communion with the Apostolic See, to the Clergy and Faithful of the Whole Catholic World, and To All Men of Good Will, on the Regulation of Birth."

"People and Events: Margaret Sanger." PBS.org. *The Pill.* 2001. Web.

Penner, Louis, et al. "Life-Threatening Disparities: The Treatment of Black and White Cancer Patients." *Journal of Social Issues: A Journal of the Society for the Psychological Study of Social Issues.* 68.2 (2012): 328–357. Print.

Petechsky, Barry. "Richard Sherman Explains What People Mean When They Call Him a Thug." *Deadspin.* 22 January 2014. Web.

Planned Parenthood. "Issue Brief: The Birth Control Pill: A History." *Planned Parenthood.* March 2013. Web.

Post Staff Reporters. "OB-GYN's Allegedly Forced Sterilization on Nearly 150 California Female Inmates." *New York Post.* 8 July 2013. Web.

Roberts, Dorothy. "Forum: Black Women and the Pill." *Family Planning Perspectives.* 32.2 (April 2000). Web.

Silber, Jeffrey, et al. "Characteristics Associated with Differences in Survival among Black and White Women with Breast Cancer." *Journal of the American Medical Association.* 310.4 (2013): 389–397. Print.

Simms, Margaret, Karina Fortuny, and Everett Henderson. "Racial and Ethnic Disparities among Low-Income Families." LIWF Fact Sheet. *Urban Institute.* August 2009.

Smith, Barbara. "Racism and Women's Studies." *Frontiers: A Journal of Women's Studies.* 5.1: 48–49. Print.

Solod, Lisa. "Marissa Mayer and the Great Class Divide." *Huffington Post.* 27 February 2013. Web.

Spelman, Elizabeth. *Inessential Women: Problems of Exclusion in Feminist Thought.* Boston: Beacon Press, 1988. Print.

Thompson, Becky. "Multiracial Feminism: Recasting the Chronology of Second Wave Feminism." *Feminist Theory Reader: Local and Global Perspectives.* Ed. Carole R. McCann and Seung-kyung Kim. 3rd ed. New York: Routledge, 2013. 56–67. Print.

Time Magazine. "A Brief History of Birth Control." *Time.* 3 May 2010. Web.

"Timeline: The Pill, 1951–1990." PBS.Org. *The Pill.* 2002. Web.

Tuchman, Gaye. "Introduction: The Symbolic Annihilation of Women by the Mass Media." *Hearth and Home: Images of Women in the Mass Media.* Ed. Gay Tuchman, Arlene Kaplan Daniels, and James Benet. New York: Oxford UP, 1978. Print.

U.S. Census Bureau. "State and County Quick Facts." 11 June 2014. Web.

United States Department of Health and Human Services. "Vital Signs: Racial Disparities in Breast Cancer Severity—United States, 2005–2009." 15 August 2014. Web.

United States Department of Labor. "Fact Sheet #28: The Family and Medical Leave Act." *Wage and Hour Division.* 25 July 2013. Web.

Wagner, Kyle. "The Word Thug was Uttered 625 Times on TV Monday." *Deadspin.* 21 January 2014. Web.

Working Mother Magazine. "Working Mother Best Companies for Hourly Workers: Executive Summary 2010." 2010. Web.

5

FEMINIST PRAXIS

Figure 5.1 AP Photo/Steubenville Herald-Star, Michael D. McElwain

Opening Illustration

In August 2012, Steubenville, Ohio, a football-driven community of approximately 20,000 residents, was rocked by accusations of the rape of a 16-year-old girl by two high school football players. During a large, alcohol-fueled party, an unconscious girl became a victim of rape, a crime that was captured by cell phone video and pictures, then circulated through social media the following day. As the *New York Times* reported,

"Twitter posts, videos and photographs circulated by some who attended the nightlong set of parties suggested that an unconscious girl had been sexually assaulted over several hours while others watched" (Macur and Schweber). The victim was not fully aware of the extent of the assault until social media reports the next day revealed more information.[1] In the insular community with a strong high school football culture, law enforcement endeavored to gather evidence of the crime as accusations surfaced. Two young men were charged with crimes relating to the events of that night. Fed up with a lack of progress and accusations of collective efforts by town leaders to suppress information and protect the perpetrators, blogger Alexandra Goddard and the hacker group **Anonymous** took action—surfacing videos, images, tweets, and other social media artifacts in an effort to collect further documentation of the crime (see Figure 5.1). A group of over a thousand people descended on Steubenville in January 2013 for a rally, where many young women, themselves residents of Steubenville, spoke movingly about having been raped.

The two young men were ultimately tried in juvenile court; they were found guilty and sentenced in March 2013. Media response to the outcome of the trial continued to fuel feminist protest, as many noted that commentators expressed undue sympathy for how the young men's lives had been ruined by their convictions.

Although Anonymous—as the vigilante hacker group calls itself—is not an explicitly feminist group, their efforts to marshal the resources provided by the Internet and social media highlight the way that activism can take myriad forms and be used to, as a *Pittsburgh Post-Gazette* editorial argued, perform "a cultural service, using their particular set of Internet tools to change some longstanding power dynamics. In a 'revenge-of-the-nerds' sort of way, Anonymous is shifting the stigma from rape victims to rape perpetrators" (Weiss). At the same time, a deeper analysis of the case reveals that these powerful technological resources need to be used very carefully, as the impulse to rush to judgment and to bring new information to light can harm as well as help. For example, Anonymous posted the transcript from the young men's probable-cause hearing but neglected to redact the victim's name.

There are many reasons why this case resonated so deeply with the public; chief among those reasons is that the tweets, texts, videos, digital pictures, and Facebook posts so clearly illustrated the fact that we live in a rape culture. The activist group FORCE: Upsetting Rape Culture defines rape culture this way: "In a rape culture, people are surrounded with images, language, laws, and other everyday phenomena that validate and perpetuate, rape. Rape culture includes jokes, TV, music, advertising, legal jargon, laws, words and imagery, that make violence against women and sexual coercion seem so normal that people believe that rape is inevitable. Rather than viewing the culture of rape as a problem to change, people in a rape culture think about the persistence of rape as 'just the way things are.'" Feminist scholars and activists together coined the term, developed and explored its meaning, and have used it over the past several decades both to diagnose the problem of the continued existence of gendered violence and to provide a basis for working to dismantle it.

Just as the facts of the Steubenville case provided a powerful reminder of the persistence of rape culture, the feminist voices of analysis and actions in response to the case show that, like FORCE, many are invested in upsetting and dismantling it. In this chapter, we explore the ways that feminist activists and educators have used a variety of sources and strategies to effect change that supports gender justice.

A Feminist Stance

- Stresses the importance of locating oneself within structures of privilege and oppression;
- Analyzes how systems of privilege and oppression operate in a number of contexts (for example, in one's personal life and relationships, in experiences of one's body, in societal institutions, etc.);
- prioritizes generating visions for social change and strategies for bringing about that change.

These visions and strategies are based on the knowledge that is generated using these foundational assumptions.

Why a Threshold Concept?
The field of Women's and Gender Studies arose out of and as a result of second-wave feminism. In fact, many early practitioners in the field

referred to it as the scholarly or academic arm of the women's movement, suggesting not just that it arose from the movement, but that it was literally a part of that social movement. Although it is now granted that the academic field and feminist social movements operate independently, the concept of praxis, defined by Berger and Radeloff as the "integration of learning with social justice," (44) is still considered central to the field. As they go on to explain, for students of Women's and Gender Studies, "Praxis is about applying one's knowledge to challenge oppressive systems and unequal traditions" (44). The same pertains to scholars in the field, as Sharlene Hesse-Biber notes in her introduction to *Feminist Research Practice:* "One of the main goals of feminist research projects is to support social justice and social transformation; these projects seek to study and to redress the many inequities and social injustices that continue to undermine and even destroy the lives of women and their families" (3). And finally, many, if not most, instructors in the field think of their teaching as itself a kind of feminist activism.

Misconception Alert

"I'm not a member of group x, so I can't be a part of their movement." Some people mistakenly think that they have to be a member of a marginalized group in order to be an advocate or activist for that cause. By this mistaken logic, men can't be feminists, and straight people can't be a part of the LGBTQ movement. Nothing could be further from the truth, however. The operative term here is "ally," which Andrea Ayvazian defines as "a member of a dominant group in our society who works to dismantle any form of oppression from which she or he receives the benefit" (724). Allies have many important roles to play in creating social change, but one of the most important, perhaps, is their role in working with other members of their dominant group. PFLAG's "Guide to Being a Straight Ally," for example, invites straight allies to "Be part of the solution even if you're not part of the GLBT community" by challenging heterosexist and homophobic comments, jokes, and stereotypes: "Whether it is around the water cooler, at a restaurant, or with your kids on the way to soccer practice, speaking up changes minds. And the more you do it, you'll find that the less your help is actually needed as people on the whole begin to change."

Framing Definitions and Related Concepts

Activism and praxis are related concepts but not synonyms. Praxis, the intersection of theory and practice, involves a visible and deliberate set of actions informed by theory, by research, and by evidence. Although most effective activism meets this definition, not all activism does. Here, we outline some of the different approaches to activism that make up feminist praxis.

Feminist action: an event or phenomenon that raises awareness and/or creates change on issues of patriarchy, gender systems, the intersectionality of identities and oppressions, and/or the overall structural inequalities experienced by women (e.g., participating in an organized event, like a protest or sit-in; raising awareness about a feminist issue through traditional and/or social media; speaking out against misogynistic beliefs; questioning institutions of power; sharing profeminist sentiments/information, etc.).

Everyday Activism

One component of feminist praxis is the notion that activism happens on a daily basis, with everyday actions that may reject or challenge oppressive practices. Jessica Valenti's *Full Frontal Feminism: A Young Woman's Guide to Why Feminism Matters* dedicates a chapter to identifying "acts of everyday feminism," ways that individual life choices can challenge oppressive practices. Regarding sex, Valenti argues that women should educate themselves, refuse to participate in "slut-bashing," take control of their sexuality, and think critically about exhibitionist behaviors. She encourages young women to critically scrutinize popular culture and mass media, and to reject misogynist male-targeted publications like *Maxim* and *Playboy*. Valenti also identifies reproductive rights as an area for everyday activism, exhorting women to take birth control, volunteer at a local clinic, find out local pharmacies' policies on providing women with birth control and emergency contraception, and call into question public attitudes that are antichoice.

Work and money, relationships, dating, guys, beauty ideals, violence against women, politics, and advocacy are all areas where everyday activism can take many forms (Valenti). In her book *A Little F'ed Up: Why Feminism Is Not a Dirty Word*, Julie Zeilinger argues that the individualization of feminism is a hallmark of the third wave, and points to an emphasis on the rejection of sexist social norms and self-acceptance in the face of societal pressure to conform to those norms.

Another related type of everyday activism is **bystander intervention**. Bystander intervention is a technique for preventing rape and sexual assault by teaching people (bystanders) to intervene when they spot a situation (on the street, at a party, in their residence hall, etc.) that seems headed in that direction. According to E. J. Graff, bystander intervention programs teach "young men and women that they can look out for others in trouble, and show them how to intervene without confrontation or danger." These programs are offered by organized activist organizations such as Men Can Stop Rape, Coaching Boys into Men, and Mentors in Violence Prevention, but the technique itself, once taught, can be modeled and practiced by individuals as they go about their everyday lives. Bystander intervention programs are a good example of praxis; social science researchers have begun to study whether they are effective, as measured by, for example, a drop in reported cases of sexual assault and rape on a campus that has instituted a program. As the results of these studies emerge, they will be used to modify existing bystander intervention programs.

Online activism: Feminist activism has increasingly moved online and has demonstrated that it can produce tangible results. Julie Zeilinger boldly claims that "The Internet is one of the greatest things ever to happen to the modern feminist movement" (140), citing its capacity for community building, organizing, and consciousness raising in particular. In terms of activism, online petitions are one prominent tactic of digital feminism. For example, a number of petitions at change.org have resulted in "victories" for women's rights, such as a petition to Sprint to change its fees for victims of domestic violence,[2] and another change. org petition launched to request that the South African government tackle the national problem of "corrective rape,"[3] or the rape of lesbians in order to convert them to heterosexuality. As a result of the petition, the South African Parliament agreed to convene a National Task Team to end the practice of "corrective" rape.

Online feminism is not without its critics, however. **Slacktivism** is a derisive term that has been coined to reflect what some have critiqued as "easy" actions that can be taken through, for example, social media, and that sometimes become a substitute for what many perceive as more demanding forms of activism such as letter-writing campaigns, lobbying legislators, protests and rallies, or other types of advocacy. With the ease of signing online petitions, posting Facebook status updates, sharing links and blogs, or **tweeting** one's views, slacktivist approaches have garnered skepticism about their effectiveness in terms of bringing about social change. Zeilinger humorously admits that it makes sense when older generations of feminists "watch us tapping away on our computers," they may think, "'Um, no, I think you're confused. That's not activism, that's actually the ancient art of sitting on your ass'" (140).

Those involved with online feminist organizing see petitions as a starting point, however, rather than an end in themselves. In "Girls Tweeting (Not Twerking) Their Way to Power," Courtney Martin refers to what is called the **ladder of engagement**, whereby "someone signs a petition, before long they're creating their own, then running a full-fledged campaign." Martin makes clear that online feminist organizing should and does distinguish between short-term and long-term "wins." For example, although a 2013 online petition pressuring Reebok to sever its endorsement deal with rapper Rick Ross was successful, there was an understanding that the broader rape culture remained intact. Martin quotes Dani McClain, who asks, "History has shown that even when a Lil Wayne or 2 Chainz is called out, norms within the industry remain and those artists quickly resume their positions at the top of the charts. How do we build a sustained effort that holds accountable the people who scout the acts, sign the deals, provide the platform and make the even bigger money?" Online activism is still in its early years, and those who are invested in it are currently doing the hard work of figuring out what both its potentials and its limitations are.

Another form of online feminist activism involves the creation and circulation of hashtags on Twitter. For example, #solidarityisforwhitewomen was created by Mikki Kendall as a way to critique the tendency of some white feminists to exclude or marginalize the issues of women of color. Writing on the blog Racialicious, blogger Lindsey Yoo argues that the hashtag "led to robust and much-needed discussions that unmasked the tendency of all progressive circles to work in silos instead of calling for *true* solidarity across multiple race and gender identities." In this instance, the hashtag was used primarily to facilitate an internal conversation among feminists to air grievances and call for change. As mentioned in Chapter 3, the #yesallwomen hashtag sprang up in the immediate aftermath of the Isla Vista, California, shootings in late May 2014, in which a young man set out on a killing spree motivated by his hatred of women, as demonstrated in videos he posted online and in a 140-page "manifesto." Within three days, 1.5 million tweets using the hashtag had been made. The #yesallwomen hashtag serves the purpose of raising consciousness and awareness about the ubiquity of sexism in our culture, and gendered violence in particular, as people wrote posts expressing their experiences of living in a patriarchal culture. According to Sasha Weiss, "There is something about the fact that Twitter is primarily designed for speech—for short, strong, declarative utterance—that makes it an especially powerful vehicle for activism, a place of liberation." In this way, Twitter is a forum with instant, global reach that is suited, to reference the title of a famous essay by Audre Lorde, to the transformation of silence into language and action. In her essay, Lorde writes, "And where the words of women are crying to be heard, we must each of us recognize our responsibility to seek those words out, to read them and share them and examine them in their pertinence to our lives" (43). Discussion in the aftermath of the Isla Vista shootings focused on how the misogynist views of the shooter, as well as the views expressed in the antifeminist men's rights online forums he frequented, are a part of the fabric of our culture. In addition, the #yesallwomen hashtag references and is intended as a retort to a sentiment expressed by those attempting to derail or dismiss feminist critiques of sexism, #notallmen.

Formal and organized activist organizations: An array of organizations, agencies, commissions, and foundations exist that illustrate the principle of feminist praxis and whose advocacy emerged from a small group of dedicated activists. Organizations are varied and emerge from a wide range of local contexts and catalysts; however, organizations galvanize around a particular issue or focus. This can be the product of a small or large group of like-minded individuals, or the brainchild of one particularly ambitious leader. For example, the National Organization for Women (NOW) emerged from the Third National Conference of Commissions on the Status of Women in 1966, where a group of similarly interested professionals, activists, and other participants discussed priorities for social justice for women. Out of that conference and the leadership of writer and activist Betty Friedan, the formal, nonprofit organization NOW was formed. Similarly, the group 9to5 originated from a small group of office workers whose gatherings to discuss sexism in the workplace led to the establishment of a formal, nonprofit group with a national policy agenda around workplace equity. Planned Parenthood, currently a network of public health clinics as well as an advocacy organization, has been around for nearly 100 years and was the product of both action and activism on the part of Margaret Sanger. More recently, INCITE!, an organization focused on combating violence against women of color, came about after a group organized a conference in 2000. The conference organizers were frustrated with feminist organizations that marginalized women of color, and so sought to fill that gap of analysis and activism. Since then, their work has expanded to include gender nonconforming and trans people of color. Their structure has multiple parts: their website lists city-based grassroots chapters of INCITE!, working groups, and affiliate groups, as well as a national collective. They also continue to host conferences around the country that bring together scholars, students, and activists who are engaged in analyzing, organizing, and mobilizing around issues of gendered violence against people of color. Many of these organizations predate the rise of Internet activism, although they almost all now have strong online presences.

Activism with limited capital: Although large-scale, organized, and formal organizations can effect change in ways that exert influence over institutions and policies, smaller-scale and locally based activism can also bring about change in local communities. A good example of this is Shelby Knox, whose local activism on the topic of comprehensive sex education versus abstinence-only education became the subject of a PBS documentary, *The Education of Shelby Knox*. As a 15-year-old high school sophomore in a Texas high school, Knox identified as a supporter of abstinence-only education and a politically conservative Southern Baptist. Over the course of the documentary period, Knox struggles to reconcile her school's abstinence-only education with the high rates of teenage pregnancy and sexually transmitted disease among her peers. Ultimately, Knox's participation in a teen group consulting with local government and an unsuccessful year-long campaign to convince the local school board to discontinue its abstinence-only sex education policy leads to her self-redefinition as a liberal Democrat. She could not accept the basic principles upon which her school's health education curriculum is founded, and eventually continued her education in college and beyond as a political science major and activist for the group change.org and its unit on organizing for activism.

Other types of activities blend these types of activism, operating with limited capital to create a formal or informal organization. At Colby College, for example, starting in 2012, student Jonathan Kalin created "Party with Consent," a movement that includes events and products that emerged counter to a series of fraternity-initiated apparel items labeled "Party with Sluts." Kalin responded by organizing social gatherings centered on critical, reflective practice:

> "I don't know how different those parties feel to students than a party that is not labeled Party With Consent, but I think that putting this language out there in the community invites people to reflect and consider, 'Am I doing the things I want to be doing? Is this consistent with the experience I want to have?' I think a big part of the movement is just posing that question," said Director of Campus Life Jed Wartman.

(Ohm)

Feminist Praxis in Women's and Gender Studies

As an academic field, Women's and Gender Studies has sought to help students cultivate an array of competencies and skills that support students' ability to link their classroom learning with their experiences outside of the classroom:

- *critical thinking*: although critical thinking is often identified as an important goal of a postsecondary education generally, Women's and Gender Studies places an especially high premium on critical approaches to everyday assumptions or "commonsense" understandings of the world. For example, in *Transforming Scholarship: Why Women's and Gender Studies Students Are Changing Themselves and the World*, Berger and Radeloff, through their interviews with WGS graduates, note that one of the most important concepts students in such programs grasp is the social construction of gender, which often involves stripping away "naturalized" ideas about men, women, gender, and sexuality, and reexamining assumptions about how gender operates both as a system and on an interpersonal level. Another example is that of privilege, oppression, and inequality. As one student wrote, "I learned that some issues I saw as personal shortcomings were actually the result of structural inequality directed at women. It also helped me to interpret the situations of other women in my family in this light. This was liberating, to say the least" (Berger and Radeloff 151). Students in Women's and Gender Studies develop the ability to strip away and "re-see" the world, calling into question previous assumptions, a foundation of critical thinking.

- *empowerment and leadership*: two interconnected features of a Women's and Gender Studies education that supports feminist praxis are students' development of what Berger and Radeloff as well as Carolyn Shrewsbury discuss as empowerment and leadership. Linking empowerment with self-confidence, Berger and Radeloff note that being empowered means being able to stand up for oneself, to challenge prevailing assumptions, and to act on one's convictions. Shrewsbury defines the women's studies classroom as built on a foundation of empowerment, or what she describes as a "concept of power as energy, capacity, and potential rather than as domination" (10). By developing self-confidence and becoming empowered to have a vision and act on that vision, students educated in Women's and Gender Studies can exercise leadership, but a particular kind of leadership that involves collaboration, responsibility, and respect. Berger and Radeloff identify the development of negotiation skills, responsibility, presentation abilities, and collaborative learning as outgrowths of a feminist education.

- *community and community engagement*: Carolyn Shrewsbury identified a sense of community in her 1993 essay "What Is Feminist Pedagogy?" as key to the feminist classroom, but it's also an important dimension of feminist praxis—developing a sense of communal identity, shared purpose, and collective values and then translating that into action in the service of those shared goals are central to the notion of community engagement. Feminist practitioners and Women's and Gender Studies students develop a sense of community identity and "build connections and relationships inside and outside of [the] workplace, family, and neighborhoods" (Berger and Radeloff 161).

- *connecting knowledge and experiences and applying knowledge for social transformation*: Amy Levin, in her 2007 report to the National Women's Studies Association summarizing assessment practices in national programs, identified the application of academic knowledge to the world outside the classroom as an important learning goal of a feminist education. Many Women's and Gender Studies classrooms incorporate an "action research" or consciousness raising project in which students are asked to do original research, engage in an advocacy or activism project, or in some other way connect the academic learning they do with the world outside the classroom. As Levin notes, successful students in Women's and Gender Studies courses are able to take what they learned—whether it's how to use an intersectional lens to approach a complex problem, how to apply standpoint theory, or a shifting understanding of gender as socially constructed— and integrate that knowledge with their own lived experiences and that of others. A current example of this kind of focus is the Know Your IX project, which is a campaign designed to both educate college students about their rights under Title IX, and empower them to advocate for change on their campuses based on what they learn about their school's compliance with Title IX (or lack thereof).

Resistance to Feminist Praxis

It is important to remember that feminist praxis, and Women's and Gender Studies education, are not embraced by all. As discussed in Chapter 1, there are those who believe that the aims of feminist movement have been achieved over the course of the last 150 years, and therefore that there is no longer a need for further feminist activism. The perpetuation of this idea that feminism is no longer needed is a form of resistance to challenging sexism and is one aspect of a phenomenon known as **backlash**. In the context of feminism, the term was popularized by journalist Susan Faludi's book of the same name, *Backlash: The Undeclared War against American Women*. Published in 1991, Faludi's book documented media and public discourse that she identified as a form of cultural backlash against the advances of the second wave of the women's movement in the 1960s and 1970s, which had been a tidal wave of social and cultural change in key areas such as workplace equality and pay equity, reproductive rights, and changing social norms around gender expectations for women. Calling into question the conclusions of media pundits and writers who claimed that feminism was to blame for women's purported ennui and dissatisfaction with their "liberation," Faludi indicts such claims as part of a larger cultural resistance to true liberation and equality for women.

Backlash against feminism continues in the 21st century, but its forms have shifted and morphed over time. In addition to overt rejection and demonization of feminism, we are now seeing what Susan J. Douglas terms "enlightened sexism," which she describes as "more nuanced and much more insidious" (11). Enlightened sexism "takes the gains of the women's movement as a given, and then uses them as permission to resurrect retrograde images of girls and women as sex objects, bimbos, and hootchie mamas still defined by their appearance and their biological destiny" (10). The nuance or subtlety that Douglas refers to comes from the fact that these retrograde images are often presented ironically, with a level of self-awareness that they're sexist, which positions the viewer or consumer of the images as in on the joke. In a post on her blog, Feminist

Frequency, entitled "Retro Sexism and Uber Ironic Advertising," Anita Sarkeesian uses the term "retro sexism" to analyze advertisements that use this type of irony, and she argues that advertisers do this in order to simultaneously present sexist images while distancing themselves from them.

According to Douglas, media stories about women **opting out** of the workforce are another aspect of enlightened sexism. A 2003 *New York Times* story, the "Opt-Out Revolution," suggested that feminism had failed in its aims to liberate women through access to education and economic self-sufficiency and that, instead, professional and educated women were returning in droves to the home, "opting out" of the hectic demands of the workplace for the halcyon sanctuary of domesticity. A range of cultural and media responses have questioned these assumptions from multiple angles. For example, an August 2013 *New York Times* story claimed, "The Opt-Out Generation Wants Back In," asserting that those women who had "opted" for domestic responsibilities over paid labor were realizing that "opting out" of careers and opting in to unpaid work subsidized by a working partner's labor was unsustainable. Article author Judith Warner uses the case study of Sheila O'Donnel to illustrate the consequences of "opting out":

> Even with the reduced schedule, the stresses of life in a two-career household put an overwhelming strain on her marriage. There were ugly fights with her husband about laundry and over who would step in when the nanny was out sick. "'All this would be easier if you didn't work,' O'Donnel recalled her husband saying. "I was so stressed," she told me. "I said, 'This is ridiculous.' We'd made plenty of money. We'd saved plenty of money." She quit her job, trading in a life of business meetings, client dinners and commissions for homework help, a "dream house" renovation and a third pregnancy. "I really thought it was what I had to do to save my marriage," she said.
>
> But the tensions in her marriage didn't improve. The couple's long-term issues of anger, jealousy and control got worse as O'Donnel's dependency grew and a sense of personal dislocation set in. Without a salary or an independent work identity, her self-confidence plummeted.

"I felt like such a loser," she said. "I poured myself into the kids and soccer. I didn't know how to deal with the downtime. I did all the volunteering, ran the auctions. It was my way . . .

Describing the case of O'Donnel, as well as the seismic economic changes since the initial "opt out" story was published in 2003, Warner claims that individual women have reconsidered their decisions in light of the personal sacrifices and uncertainty and dependence that such a "choice" engenders.

A second perspective is offered in the story "Mothers Are Not 'Opting Out'—They Are Out of Options," in which Sara Kendzior critiques the restrictive and inadequate supports for working women and dual-career couples who hope to have successful work lives as well as fulfilling family lives. As Kendzior argues, "The assumed divide between mothers who work inside and outside the home is presented as a war of priorities.[4] But in an economy of high debt and sinking wages, nearly all mothers live on the edge. Choices made out of fear are not really choices. The illusion of choice is a way to blame mothers for an economic system rigged against them. There are no 'mommy wars,'[5] only money wars—and almost everyone is losing."

Finally, a number of feminist theorists and critics have argued that the current cultural obsession with girls' and women's physical appearance in terms of the shape, size, and sexiness of their bodies is a form of backlash against feminism. Gender norms for girls and women have inarguably changed in significant ways over the past 50 years as a result of feminism, but even as women have greater freedoms in many areas of life, there is a corresponding greater scrutiny of their bodies. Sandra Bartky, for example, points out that "Women are no longer required to be chaste or modest, to restrict their sphere of activity to the home, or even to realize their properly feminine destiny in maternity." Instead, she argues, "normative femininity is coming more and more to be centered on woman's body—not its duties and obligations or even its capacity to bear children, but its sexuality, more precisely, its presumed heterosexuality and its appearance" (41–42). Further, Bartky argues that the latter type of control only started to assume greater importance as the former waned as a result of feminist struggles to redefine women's roles.

Jessica Valenti calls it a distraction: "The more we're worked up about how fat we are or how hot we want to be, the less we're worried about the things that really matter, the things that will affect our lives" (199–200). Naomi Wolf's 1991 book *The Beauty Myth: How Images of Beauty Are Used against Women*, argued that "The qualities that a given period calls beautiful in women are merely symbols of the female behavior that that period considers desirable: *The **beauty myth** is always actually prescribing behavior and not appearance*" (14); in other words, reorienting women's attention to their physical appearances is as much about directing women's behavior and time as it is surveilling their appearances and conformity to a narrowly defined ideal of female beauty.

A related term is **postfeminism,** which rests on the premise that the aims of feminist movement(s) have been achieved and that we live in a society where women experience a full range of choices equal to those of men, or as Angela McRobbie explains, "post-feminism positively draws on and invokes feminism as that which can be taken into account, to suggest that equality is achieved, in order to install a whole repertoire of new meanings which emphasise that it is no longer needed" (255). Another definition uses postfeminism interchangeably or as an alternate to the term "backlash."

Misconception Alert

White men are frequently victims of "reverse discrimination." One misconception about feminism and feminist movement is that not only have the goals of feminist movement been achieved, but that in fact women have distinct advantages over men, or that men are significantly disadvantaged by women's achievements or by affirmative action and equity efforts. As a brief review of key issues shows, in fact reverse discrimination is uncommon, partly because, by using a macro lens as outlined in Chapter 3, we can see how systems of privilege and oppression interact to grant some groups privileges and withhold them from others. In this system, white men are usually an advantaged group. In this sense, feminism in the popular imagination is at odds on some key issues with the demographic and statistical realities of women's lives in the United States and internationally.

Although there have been important achievements in improving the quality of life for many women in the United States and internationally, demographic and statistical realities reveal that, in fact, there is a good deal of work to be done to bring about gender equity, particularly because such claims about feminism having reached its goals typically operate under the assumption that the goals of middle-class, white women are the goals of feminist movement. However, feminist movement takes many forms and serves a broad spectrum of women's needs. For example:

- Women and girls globally experience high rates of violence and cultural sexism ranging from son preference to dowry deaths to sex-selective abortion.
- Female circumcision, the nonmedical removal of all or part of a women's genitalia, persists across many parts of Africa, Asia, North America, and Europe.
- Males outnumber females 3 to 1 in family films. In contrast, females make up just over 50% of the population in the United States. Even more staggering is the fact that this ratio, as seen in family films, is the same as it was in 1946 (Geena Davis Institute on Gender and Media).
- As UNICEF reports, women are dramatically underrepresented in national representative and legislative bodies, making up just 17% of elected representatives, and 6% of heads of state.
- Although women have made substantial gains in efforts for economic justice, wage inequalities continue to persist. According to 9to5.org, an advocacy organization for women workers, "a significant pay gap exists for women and people of color. Women earn 77 cents for every dollar earned by men in 2011 annual earnings. For women of color the gap is even wider—African-American women earn only 69 cents and Latinas just 60 cents for every dollar earned by males, the highest earners" (9to5). Legislative efforts such as the Paycheck Fairness Act aim to reduce this gap, but women still make less than their male coworkers.
- As the National Center for Education Statistics explains, "Title IX of the Education Amendments of 1972 protects people from dis-

crimination based on sex in education programs and activities that receive federal financial assistance." As a result of this legislative act, there is some cultural perception that equity for women in athletics has led to inequities or disadvantages for men. However, the Women's Sports Foundation explains that, in fact, men's participation in athletics is increasing; they observe: "This misinformation campaign takes the focus away from the facts that (1) women continue to be significantly underrepresented among high school and college athletes, (2) the gap between men's and women's sports participation and support is not closing and (3) it is the wealthiest athletic programs in NCAA Division I-A that are dropping men's minor sports, typically because they are shifting these monies to compete in the football and men's basketball arms race" (Women's Sports Foundation). On the whole, female athletes receive fewer scholarship dollars ($965 million female vs. $1.15 billion male) and fewer athletic participation opportunities (3.2 million female vs. 4.5 million male) than male athletes. A news story in the *Christian Science Monitor* reveals the more common explanation for the elimination of men's sports: "The NCAA also points out that nonrevenue men's sports are often cut to provide more funds for the two big revenue sports, football and basketball. In 2006, for instance, Rutgers University dropped men's tennis, a team with a budget of approximately $175,000. The National Women's Law Center points out that Rutgers spent about $175,000 in the same year on hotel rooms for the football team—for home games."

Anchoring Topics through the Lens of Feminist Praxis

Work and Family

Several organizations have emerged from large-scale or small-scale **grassroots activism** to achieve economic justice for all women. In this section, we highlight the work of several organizations whose efforts have brought about or influenced policy and practice changes.

MomsRising: serves as a kind of clearinghouse that takes multiple approaches to activism on behalf of women. They are focused on a range of issues including maternity and paternity leave, flexible work options, health care access, early childhood education, and paid sick leave. Since 2006, the group has been engaged in organizing grassroots activists, for example, providing online resources for lobbying legislators to support fair wages or family leave. MomsRising also hosts a blog where women can share their stories on the topics supported by the organization; it also aims to "amplify women's voices and issues in the national dialogue and in the media" in order to advocate for positive social and legislative change that will support work–life balance.

9to5: The organization 9to5 emerged in 1973 when the average workplace was plagued by sexism and sexist practices ranging from lack of job protections for women who became pregnant, a lack of recourse for women workers experiencing sexual harassment, and inequities in pay. This group has grown over the last four decades to support a range of national legislative efforts. For example, 9to5 supported national policy achievements such as the 1978 Pregnancy Discrimination Act, which protects the jobs of women workers who require time off to accommodate a pregnancy; the Family and Medical Leave Act of 1993 (FMLA) that allows for 12 weeks of unpaid leave to accommodate childbirth, illness, or the care of a family member; and the Lilly Ledbetter Fair Pay Act of 2009 which changed the statute of limitations to allow for more time for workers who have experienced wage discrimination to file a compensatory lawsuit. The organization advocates for family-supporting jobs, for workplace flexibility including measures like paid family leave and paid sick leave, and for equal opportunities in the workplace such as greater accountability measures for cases of discrimination and harassment.

National Organization for Women: One of the most established women's organizations in the United States, the National Organization for Women was formed in 1966 and has maintained a focus on its initial goal: "To take action to bring women into full participation in the mainstream of American society now, assuming all the privileges and responsibilities thereof in truly equal partnership with men" (National Organization for Women). Over its four decades of activism, NOW has agitated on behalf of the Title IX Education Amendments supporting equality in education and athletics, advocated for the Equal Rights Amendment, supported the establishment of rape crisis centers, and supported women's right to safe, legal abortion.

Language, Images, and Symbols

Although critical to the development of social norms and assumptions around gender, language, images, and symbols can be particularly challenging to reshape. Unlike work and family or reproductive rights—which are often subject at least in part to public policy (whether laws, regulations, funding priorities, initiatives, etc.), symbolic representations of gender in the form of art, music, popular culture, literature, film, are much less subject to such forms of social and political legislation, and so activists around language, images, and symbols take different approaches to critiquing, reframing, and influencing symbolic representations of women and gender.

One group, active since the 1980s, is the Guerrilla Girls. Following an exhibit at the Museum of Modern Art on "An International Survey of Painting and Sculpture," protests about the white, male, Eurocentric and U.S.-centric content of the "international survey" emerged. Feminists in the art world critiqued the exclusion of women and people of color from important temporary exhibits such as these, and that critique broadened out to include an analysis of whose work was included in museums' permanent collections and exhibited in commercial galleries. They created colorful, sarcastic, and humorous posters and posted them as a way to draw attention to the art world's gender and racial disparity. As the group themselves explains, the Guerrilla Girls are

> a bunch of anonymous females who take the names of dead women artists as pseudonyms and appear in public wearing gorilla masks. We have produced posters, stickers, books, printed projects, and actions that expose sexism and racism in politics, the art world, film and the culture at large. We use humor to convey information, provoke discussion, and show that feminists can be funny. We wear gorilla masks to focus on the issues rather than our personalities. Dubbing ourselves the conscience of culture, we declare ourselves feminist counterparts to the mostly male tradition of anonymous do-gooders like Robin Hood, Batman, and the Lone Ranger. Our work has been passed around the world by kindred spirits who we are proud to have as supporters. It has also appeared in *The New York Times*, *The Nation*, *Bitch* and *Bust*; on TV and radio, including NPR, the BBC and CBC; and in countless art and feminist texts.

The mystery surrounding our identities has attracted attention. We could be anyone; we are everywhere.

Highlighting the exclusion of women artists and artists of color from mainstream galleries, the loosely organized group engages in a range of activities from demonstrations to "flash mob" type protests, to billboards and posters as well as authoring books and public letters.

Founded in 2004 by actress Geena Davis, the Institute on Gender and Media takes a three-pronged approach to changing the "media landscape" around gender representations, including research, education, and advocacy. First, as the sponsor of research studies, the organization is able to support investigations into media representations, providing a sound and robust empirical foundation for its education and advocacy. For example, the institute has sponsored studies of industry leaders' perceptions of gender in family films, into gender disparities both on-screen and behind the camera, and assessments of the portrayal of occupations in G-rated, family films. Such research investigations have allowed the institute to draw important conclusions, for example, about the representation of women in particular fields, such as the finding that in one study, not a single female character was depicted in medical science, executive business, or politics (Smith 2). The institute uses this research in two equally important ways. First, the institute and its organizational partners seek to educate stakeholders and leaders about the impact of gender representations in media. In other words, the institute reaches out to the *makers* of media in an attempt to shape the content that they produce. They also reach out to *consumers* of media; the institute offers an array of web-based resources including lessons and curricula that can be used by teachers in a variety of settings to teach critical thinking and media literacy skills to young people. Finally, the institute engages in advocacy by providing public presentations, consulting with professional and industry groups, using social media, and interfacing and partnering with other organizations such as UN Women and the Girl Scouts.

Feminist praxis can take other forms around symbolic representation—such as the #notbuyingit Twitter campaign initiated by *Missrepresentation.org*, a nonprofit social action campaign and media organization emerging from the documentary of the same name, written and directed by Jennifer Siebel Newsom. *Miss Representation* focused on making visible the underrepresentation and degrading representations of women in the media. The #notbuyingit campaign is one way that organizations can use social media to highlight, critique, and mobilize action about symbolic representation, in this case, products that offer stereotyped, degrading, or harmful messages. For example, an August 2013 tweet highlighted an Etsy product, a glass with the message "You've Just Been Roofied," that reveals itself at the bottom after the drinker has finished the beverage. One of the goals of the campaign is to call attention to such products and hold manufacturers accountable for misogynist products as well as to discourage consumers from purchasing them.

Bodies

A key focus of feminist activism has been the idea that women have a right to control their own bodies. There is a long history of feminist organizing around the issues of rape, sexual assault, and street harassment. In its earliest forms, this activism focused on marital violence and was sometimes linked to the temperance movement, as many saw alcohol as the chief cause of men's violence against their wives and children. It was not until the second wave of feminism, however, that the impact of feminist efforts began to be felt. A brief discussion of this activism over the past 40 years reveals both continuity and change in terms of its targets, tone, tactics and strategies.

A well-established form of activism around violence against women is the international movement, Take Back the Night. Starting in 1976 in Brussels, Belgium, this activist effort uses marches, protests, and demonstrations as well as candlelight vigils and accompanying speakers to call for the elimination of violence against women. Take Back the Night marches are a symbolic reclamation of public space after dark, which girls and women are taught to fear through the messages they receive about their responsibility in protecting themselves against attack. The Take Back the Night Foundation, established in 1999, describes its goals as follows: "The Take Back The Night Foundation seeks to end sexual assault, domestic violence, dating violence, sexual abuse and all other forms of sexual violence. We serve to create safe communities and respectful relationships through awareness events and initiatives"

("About"). Take Back the Night marches are especially prevalent on college campuses, where they continue to play a crucial role in raising young people's awareness of these issues and also provide a powerful forum for survivors to speak and heal. Critiques of the movement have centered on the potential implication that "stranger rape" and nighttime attacks in the bushes are the primary form of sexual violence against women, when in fact a small minority of sexual assaults are committed by someone unknown to the victim.

Similar in its goals but different in its tone and tactics is the **Slut-Walk** movement. SlutWalks began after a police officer at a safety forum at York University in January 2011 claimed that women "should avoid dressing like sluts in order not to be victimized." Outraged, a grassroots and social media campaign led by Heather Jarvis and Sonya Barnett emerged in major cities across the United States and Canada in which thousands took to the streets with chants and signs to protest the victim-blaming attitude reflected in Constable Michael Sanguinetti's comments. Even though the officer later apologized, his comments set off hundreds of organized SlutWalks, starting with the April 3 march in Toronto. The foundation of SlutWalk is the rejection of the idea that women's sexuality, sexual behavior, or sexual expression is the cause of sexual violence against women or of rape culture. Marchers come together in their rejection and condemnation of victim blaming. As founder Jarvis recalled: "The idea that there is some aesthetic that attracts sexual assault or even keeps you safe from sexual assault is inaccurate, ineffective and even dangerous." She recalled a sign at the march that read: "It was Christmas day. I was 14 and raped in a stairwell wearing snowshoes and layers. Did I deserve it too?" (Stampler) Many participants in such walks choose to wear "provocative" or revealing outfits as a way of embracing, co-opting, and challenging the term "slut," which attaches negative value to women who engage in sexual activity. Jessica Valenti commented on the emergence of SlutWalks as a way of challenging assumptions about female sexuality and male entitlement: "Women deserve to be safe from violent assault, no matter what they wear. And the sad fact is, a miniskirt is no more likely to provoke a rapist than a potato sack is to deter one." SlutWalks proved to be controversial, even among feminists, however, in part because some feminists reject the idea that "slut" can be co-opted or repurposed because of its sexist and patriarchal origins. Rebecca Traister, for example, wrote that "Scantily clad marching seems weirdly blind to the race, class, and body-image issues that usually (rightly) obsess young feminists and seems inhospitable to scads of women who, for various reasons, might not feel it logical or comfortable to expression their revulsion at victim-blaming by donning bustiers. So whereas the mission of SlutWalks is crucial, the package is confusing and leaves young feminists open to the very kinds of attacks they are battling." Many women of color also pointed out that because of racialized stereotypes that construct them as hypersexualized, they have an even more ambivalent relationship to the term "slut."

A controversial activist strategy related to combating rape and sexual assault is the practice of posting (physically and/or virtually) the names of alleged perpetrators. In the past, names might have been posted on a photocopied flyer and posted in women's restrooms or in residence halls on campus, whereas now the names might circulate online. In spring of 2014 an unknown person or persons posted a list of four names under the heading "Rapists on Campus" around the campus of Columbia University. The act received national attention, in large part because Columbia was already in the news as a result of 23 students filing a federal complaint against the university alleging the mishandling of sexual assault cases. According to CNN, the complaint alleges "the Ivy League university discouraged students from reporting sexual assaults, allowed perpetrators to remain on campus, sanctioned inadequate disciplinary actions for perpetrators and discriminated against students based on their sexual orientation." Whereas some defended this approach as a way of empowering students to protect themselves when the university administration had failed to do so, others rightly pointed out this tactic's potential for abuse.

Another way that feminist activism around violence has changed in the last 40 years is that it increasingly includes (and is sometimes led by) men. The White Ribbon Campaign, based in Canada, describes itself as the "world's largest movement of men and boys working to end violence against women and girls, promote gender equity, healthy relationships and a new vision of masculinity." Primarily educational in its focus, the White Ribbon Campaign offers workshops, conferences, and trainings.

An organization whose focus is more parallel to Take Back the Night and SlutWalks is Walk a Mile in Her Shoes, which is an international men's march that features men walking in high heels. While lauded for raising men's awareness of gendered violence and facilitating their active involvement in the movement against it, this event has been criticized for not always being thoughtful about the way it is organized and advertised. More specifically, some local marches have played up the idea that men walking in "women's" shoes is funny, thereby reinforcing rather than challenging traditional constructions of masculinity. One response to this is for march organizers to challenge attendees' assumptions by reminding them that not all women wear heels, and not all who wear heels are women. Another example is the activist group Men Can Stop Rape, a nonprofit organization engaging in education programs, awareness building campaigns, and training projects with the goal of combating men's violence against women. The organization "mobilizes men to use their strength for creating cultures free from violence, especially men's violence against women," and operates from the assumption that men are "vital allies with the will and character to make healthy choices and foster safe, equitable relationships" ("What We Do"). Their 2014 "Take a Stand" campaign provides strategies for bystander intervention—ways men (and women) can support women who are in uncomfortable or dangerous situations (see Figure 5.2 for an example of an public awareness campaign of this nature).

Activism around street harassment has further gained new visibility in recent years as a result of the creation of **Hollaback**. Hollaback, which is described as a "non-profit and movement to end street harassment," is a good example of activism that has been enhanced by technological innovation. According to the website, "At Hollaback!, we leverage technology to bring voice to an issue that historically has been silenced, and to build leadership within this movement to break the silence." It was inspired by one woman who was so fed up by her experience of street harassment that she decided to take out her phone and snap a picture of the man who was masturbating on the subway while staring at her. She initially took her complaint to the police, but they did nothing, so she posted the photo online, and the story eventually got considerable media attention. In response, a group of

Figure 5.2 Men Can Stop Rape (www.mencanstoprape.org)

young people decided to start a blog where people could share their experiences of street harassment. From there, the project has grown to include the creation and dissemination of a mobile app that people can use to document the nature and location of street harassment. On an individual level, it can be empowering for someone who has experienced harassment to fight back by documenting their experience and connecting with others who have had similar experiences. On a broader level, to do so also contributes to the collection of data that can be used when approaching police and policy makers about addressing the issue. Importantly, Hollaback employs an intersectional approach to street harassment, rightly pointing out that street harassment can be "sexist, racist, transphobic, homophobic, ableist, sizeist and/or classist. It is an expression of the interlocking and overlapping oppressions we face and it functions as a means to silence our voices and 'keep us in our place.'"

Case Study: The Spark Movement

In 2010, the American Psychological Association published the "Report of the APA Task Force on the Sexualization of Young Girls," the results of work conducted by a subcommittee of the national organization of the field of psychology. The group was charged as follows:

> examine and summarize the best psychological theory, research, and clinical experience addressing the sexualization of girls via media and other cultural messages, including the prevalence of these messages and their impact on girls, and include attention to the role and impact of race/ethnicity and socioeconomic status. The Task Force will produce a report, including recommendations for research, practice, education and training, policy, and public awareness.

Defining early sexualization as the objectification of girls and women, exclusive value attached to the sexual attributes of individuals, and inappropriate imposition of sexuality on a person, the group's report documented the ample evidence of sexualization of young girls, as well as the cognitive, emotional, psychological, and physical harms caused by early sexualization. The group made recommendations for future direction for research, public policy, practice, education, and training, and as a result of that report, the Spark Movement emerged.

The Spark Movement describes itself as "a girl-fueled activist movement to demand an end to the sexualization of women and girls in media. We're collaborating with hundreds of girls 13–22 and more than 60 national organizations to reject the commodified, sexualized images of girls in media and support the development of girls' healthy sexuality and self-esteem." The movement illustrates feminist praxis because of its blending of research, education, training, and "everyday activism," such as publicly critiquing through protest, social media, or other methods those products that objectify, stereotype, and demean girls and women. Some of the organization's victories include launching a Change.org petition asking *Seventeen Magazine* to include at least one photo spread each issue that included "unaltered images." The petition entitled "Give Girls Images of Real Girls!" was ultimately delivered to *Seventeen*'s editor; a 2012 update from the petition initiator, Julie Bluhm, reported that "Seventeen listened! They're saying they won't use photoshop to digitally alter their models! This is a huge victory, and I'm so unbelievably happy" (Bluhm).

The Spark Movement directs activist efforts through its research blog, recommendations for taking action (such as a recent fundraising campaigns directed at supporting girl activists), and documenting efforts to intervene in harmful practices or correcting gaps in education and training (such as a national effort to educate athletic coaches about sexual assault prevention). The work of the Spark Movement illustrates how activism can emerge from research and inform policy and practice.

Misconception Alert

I'm only one person and can't make a difference, being an activist is a full-time job, activism is all about marching in the streets. When taking a Women's and Gender Studies course, students sometimes feel overwhelmed and unsure how to take action. As this chapter demonstrates, however, there are large and small-scale activist efforts that any one individual can take—and that *allies* are critical to the achievement of social justice.

End of Chapter Elements

Evaluating Prior Knowledge

1. Think about past educational experiences you've had in school. To what degree have you seen intersections between your classroom learning, or academic knowledge, and your lived experience? Which classes most commonly "translated" into your nonschool life? Which seemed disconnected?

Application Exercises

1. Spend a day paying careful attention to gender dynamics in your own life—to interactions with friends, family, and coworkers; to your workplace culture, practices, or discourse; to your own use of language and ways of communicating. Framing your discussion in terms of feminist praxis, reflect on how you see threshold concepts from the texts manifested in your everyday experiences and how you might engage in "everyday activism."

2. Visit the website of one of the following organizations. In what ways do you see the organization engaged in feminist praxis?
    a. http://9to5.org/
    b. www.now.org/
    c. www.feministfrequency.com/
    d. www.guerrillagirls.com/
    e. www.ihollaback.org/
    f. http://upsettingrapeculture.com/
    g. www.womensmediacenter.com
    h. http://upsettingrapeculture.com/

Skills Assessment/Check for Understanding

1. Think about the key terms presented in this chapter, including feminist praxis, ally, backlash, rape culture, postfeminism, and activism. Which of these have you used previously in your everyday vocabulary? Which take on new meanings in the context of this chapter material?

2. Select an antifeminist or profeminist website and thoroughly explore the site, paying attention to both the content of the site and how the

site functions. Answer the following short-answer prompts with several paragraphs each, drawing on specific examples from the website.

a. Summarize the overall point-of-view of the website.

b. How does the website connect to a broader feminist movement?

c. What opportunities for activism/action beyond reading does the website offer?

d. How does the website situate feminism within a broader framework of interlocking oppressions/intersectionality?

e. Describe how the website acknowledges the social construction of gender, privilege, and oppression (or resists such a construction).

f. Describe the role that community and/or collaboration plays in the website. Is it supported or acknowledged? Is it suggested as a value?

g. Analyze the persona of the website—that is, analyze the tone, mood, and "personality" of the website. Here, you should draw from both visual and textual cues that contribute to the overall persona of the website.

h. Finally, drawing on your previous answers, evaluate the website's effectiveness as an antifeminist or profeminist site. This answer should be longer than your previous answers, and should synthesize the elements from questions a through g.

Discussion Questions

1. Think about some of the recommendations made throughout this chapter for small- and large-scale activism. Are there ways that you have engaged in activism? Describe your previous experiences.

2. What are the major barriers or challenges to social change? What are the major barriers or challenges to your personal involvement in activism for gender justice?

3. One of the goals of a feminist perspective is "the importance of locating oneself within structures of privilege and oppression" and to "analyze" how systems of privilege and oppression operate in a number of contexts (for example, in one's personal life and relationships, in experiences of one's body, in societal institutions, etc.). How does your personal social location connect to a larger social structure? What forms of feminist praxis would be most appropriate and com-

fortable for you to engage in, based on that location? Which would be uncomfortable and why?

Writing Prompts

1. Feminist praxis is the ability to apply and/or enact feminist theoretical principles to your own life and experience. Create a self-reflection or narrative that demonstrates your participation in and analysis of a feminist event or act of social change of which you were a part. This will include supporting documentation (e.g., photos, documents, Internet coverage) of the event/action. Write a personal narrative reflection describing and analyzing a particular experience/event/action in which you have participated that meets the criteria of feminism action.

   > feminist action: an event or phenomenon that raises awareness and/or creates change on issues of patriarchy, gender systems, the intersectionality of identities and oppressions, and/or the overall structural inequalities experienced by women (e.g., participating in an organized event, like a protest or sit-in; raising awareness about a feminist issue through traditional and/or social media; speaking out against misogynistic beliefs; questioning institutions of power; sharing pro-feminist sentiments/information).

2. Collect and assemble a series of artifacts that document your participation in this event. Write an essay in which you:
   a. explain the event
   b. explain/describe your documentation and how they represent the event
   c. describe your role in the event
   d. address your perception of the outcome of the event
   e. connect your experience in this event to the definition of feminist action

Notes

1 www.nytimes.com/2012/12/17/sports/high-school-football-rape-case-unfolds-online-and-divides-steubenville-ohio.html?pagewanted=all&_r=1&
2 www.change.org/petitions/sprint-improve-policies-to-keep-domestic-violence-victims-safe
3 www.change.org/petitions/south-africa-take-action-to-stop-corrective-rape

4   www.nytimes.com/2013/06/11/opinion/the-mommy-wars-time-to-call-a-truce.html
5   www.amazon.com/Mommy-Wars-Stay-at-Home-Choices-Families/dp/
    0812974484

Works Cited and Suggested Readings

9to5.org. "*Paycheck Fairness Act.*" 9to5.org. 25 August 2013. Web.

"About Take Back the Night." *Take Back the Night.org.* 2013. 26 August 2013.Web.

"About: What is Hollaback?" *Hollaback! You Have the Power to End Street Harassment.* 2014. 28 May 2014. Web.

APA Task Force on the Sexualization of Young Girls. "Report of the Task Force on the Sexualization of Young Girls." *American Psychological Association.* 2010. Web.

Ayvazian, Andrea. "Interrupting the Cycle of Oppression: The Role of Allies as Agents of Change." *Race, Class, and Gender in the United States: An Integrated Study.* Paula Rothenberg, ed. 7th ed. New York: Worth, 724–730. Print.

Bartky, Sandra. "Foucault, Feminism, and the Modernization of Patriarchal Power." *The Politics of Women's Bodies.* Ed. Rose Weitz. New York: Oxford UP, 1998. 25–45. Print.

Baumgardner, Jennifer, and Amy Richards. *Grassroots: A Field Guide for Feminist Activism.* New York: Farrar, Strauss, and Giroux, 2004. Print.

Baxandall, Rosalyn, and Linda Gordon, eds. *Dear Sisters: Dispatches from the Women's Liberation Movement.* New York: Basic Books, 2001. Print.

Berger, Michele, and Cheryl Radeloff. *Transforming Scholarship; Why Women's and Gender Studies Students Are Changing Themselves and the World.* New York: Routledge, 2011. Print.

Bluhm, Julia. "*Seventeen Magazine*: Give Girls Images of Real Girls!" *Change.org.* July 2012. Web.

Collins, Patricia Hill. *On Intellectual Activism.* Philadelphia: Temple UP, 2012. Print.

Crook, Lawrence. "Alleged 'Rapist List' Appears around Columbia University." CNN. com. 15 May 2014. Web.

Douglas, Susan J. *Enlightened Sexism: The Seductive Message that Feminism's Work is Done.* New York: Henry Holt, 2010. Print.

The Education of Shelby Knox. Dir. Marion Lipschitz and Rose Rosenblatt. Women Make Movies. 2005. Film.

Faludi, Susan. *Backlash: The Undeclared War against American Women.* New York: Crown, 1991. Print.

Feinberg, JonaRose Jaffe. "Postfeminism." In *The Women's Movement Today: An Encyclopedia of Third-Wave Feminism.* Ed. Leslie Heywood. Westport, CT: Greenwood P, 2006. Print.

Finley, Laura, and Emily Reynolds Stringer. *Beyond Burning Bras: Feminist Activism for Everyone.* Santa Barbara, CA: Praeger, 2010. Print.

Geena Davis Institute on Gender in the Media. "Research Informs and Empowers." *SeeJane.org.* 27 May 2014. Web.

Goodale, Gloria. "40 Years Later, Title IX Is Still Fighting Perception It Hurts Men's Sports." *Christian Science Monitor.* 23 June 2012. Web.

Graff, E. J. "Building a Respect Culture." *American Prospect.* 9 January 2013. Web.

Guerrilla Girls. "Guerrilla Girls: Reinventing the 'F' Word: Feminism." 2011. Web.

Hernandez, Daisy, and Bushra Rehman, eds. *Colonize This!: Young Women of Color on Today's Feminism.* Berkeley, CA: Seal P, 2002. Print.

Hesse-Biber, Sharlene. "Introduction." *Feminist Research Practice: A Primer.* Thousand Oaks, CA: 2014. Print.

INCITE!: Women of Color against Violence, eds. *Color of Violence: The INCITE! Anthology.* Cambridge, MA: South End P, 2006.

Kacmarek, Julia, and Elizabeth Geffre. "Rape Culture Is: You Know It When You See It." *Huffington Post.* 1 June 2013. Web.

Kendzior, Sarah. "Mothers Are Not 'Opting Out'—They Are Out of Options." *Al Jazeera.* 19 August 2013. Web.

Levin, Amy. *Questions for a New Century: Women's Studies and Integrative Learning, a Report to the National Women's Studies Association.* 2007. Web.

Lorde, Audre. *Sister Outsider.* Trumansburg, NY: Crossing P, 1984. Print.

Macur, Juliet and Nate Schweber. "Rape Case Unfolds on Web and Splits City." *New York Times.* 16 December 2012. Web.

Marcotte, Amanda. *Get Opinionated: A Progressive's Guide to Finding Your Voice (and Taking a Little Action).* Berkeley, CA: Seal P, 2010. Print.

Martin, Courtney E. "Girls Tweeting (Not Twerking) Their Way to Power." *New York Times.* 4 September 2013. Web.

McRobbie, Angela. "Post-Feminism and Popular Culture." *Feminist Media Studies.* 4.3 (2004): 255–264. Web.

National Center for Education Statistics. "Fast Facts: Title IX." *Institute of Education Sciences.* 2011. 27 August 2013. Web.

National Organization for Women. "Founding: Setting the Stage." 3 June 2013. Web.

Ohm, Rachel. "Colby Student's 'Party with Consent' Gets the Nod at 30 Campuses." *Portland Press Herald.* 25 Thursday 2014. Web.

Parents and Friends of Lesbians and Gays. "Guide to Being a Straight Ally." pflag.org. 2007. Web.

Rush, Curtis. "Cop Apologizes for 'Sluts' Remark at Law School." *Toronto Star.* 18 February 2011. Web.

Sarkeesian, Anita. "Retro Sexism and Uber Ironic Advertising." *Feminist Frequency.* Web.

Shrewsbury, Carolyn. "What Is Feminist Pedagogy?" *Women's Studies Quarterly.* 3.4 (1993): 8–16. Web.

Smith, Stacy L., Marc Choueiti, and Jessica Stern. "Occupational Aspirations: What Are G-Rated Films Teaching Children about the World of Work?" *Geena Davis Institute on Gender in Media.* 2012. Web.

Spark Movement. "About Us." *Sparksummit.* 2013. Web. 26 August 2013.

Stampler, Laura. "SlutWalks Sweep the Nation." *Huffington Post.* 20 April 2011. Web.

Stewart, Nikki Ayanna. "Transform the World: What You Can Do with a Degree in Women's Studies." *Ms.* Spring 2007: 65–66. Print.

Sullivan, J. Courtney, and Courtney E. Martin. *Click: When We Knew We Were Feminists.* New York: Perseus Books, 2010. Print.

Traister, Rebecca. "Ladies, We Have a Problem." *New York Times.* 20 July 2011. Web.

UNICEF. The State of the World's Children: Women and Children, The Double Dividend of Gender Equality. 2007. 26 August 2013. Web.

Valenti, Jessica. *Full Frontal Feminism: A Young Woman's Guide to Why Feminism Matters.* Berkeley, CA: Seal P, 2007. Print.

——. "SlutWalks and the Future of Feminism." *Capital Times.* 8 June 2011. Web.

Warner, Judith. "The Opt-Out Generation Wants Back In." *New York Times.* 7 August 2013. Web.

Weiss, Joanna. "Anonymous in Steubenville: Can Secret Avengers Use the Internet to Bring Justice in a Rape Case?" *Pittsburgh Post-Gazette*. 10 January 2013. Web.

Weiss, Sasha. "The Power of #yesallwomen." *New Yorker.* 26 May 2014. Web.

"What We Do: Our Mission and Vision." *Men Can Stop Rape.* 5 June 2014. Web.

White Ribbon Australia. "White Ribbon Australia: Fact Sheet 1—Origin of the Campaign." 26 May 2014. Web.

Wolf, Naomi. *The Beauty Myth: How Images of Beauty Are Used against Women.* New York: HarperCollins, 1991. Print.

Women's Sports Foundation. "Title IX Myths and Facts." 2011. 24 August 2013. Web.

Yoo, Lindsey. "Solidarity Is for White Women and Asian People Are Funny." *Racialicious: The Intersection of Race and Pop Culture.* 27 August 2013. Web.

Zeilinger, Julie. *A Little F'd Up: Why Feminism Is Not a Dirty Word.* Berkeley, CA: Seal P, 2012. Print.

Glossary/Index

#notallmen: A Twitter hashtag created by men's rights activists to contradict the effort to make visible and to critique sexism and violence 97, 161

#notbuyingit 173–4

#yesallwomen: A Twitter hashtag created in response to #notallmen to call out misogynist violence and sexism 97, 160–1

ableism: Institutionalized practices and individual actions and beliefs that posit the able-bodied as the norm. It works to promote negative images of disabled women, such as the myth that it is not possible for someone with a disability to have a positive and equal relationship 73, 115

abstinence-only sex education 162

act-like-a-man box: Paul Kivel's articulation of masculine gender norms and expectations that men are socialized to adhere to 44–5, 128

activism: Conscious efforts to raise awareness about a social problem and and/or to bring about social change 10, 11, 12,13, 14, 116, 117, 135, 154, 156, 157–9, 160, 161–2, 164, 165, 170, 171, 174, 176, 177, 180

Adair, Vivyan 132; "Branded with Infamy" 130–1

Adams, Natalie Guice 37

Affordable Healthcare Act 91

Aid to Families with Dependent Children 92

Alger, Horatio 82

All the Women Are White, All the Blacks Are Men, But Some of Us Are Brave 116

Allen, Paula Gunn: *The Sacred Hoop* 12

allies: Defined by Andrea Ayvazian as "a member of a dominant group in our society who works to dismantle any form of oppression from which she or he receives the benefit." 7, 10, 72,156, 177, 180

Allstate Foundation: 2014 Teens and Personal Finance Survey 33

Amateur International Boxing Association 113

American Beauty 35, 36

American Psychological Association 179

American Student Government Association 39

American University 40

187